W9-CBX-388

IRELAND

The Edge of Europe

IRELAND

The Edge of Europe

Arnold Dobrin

THOMAS NELSON INC.
New York   Camden

All photographs are from the Irish Tourist Board except the following from: Aer Lingus, p. 48; British Tourist Authority, p. 165; Camera Press Ltd., p. 121 (top); Irish Times, p. 122; Lensmen House, p. 74; National Library of Ireland, pp. 34, 121, 125, 128, 129, 146, 147, 150, 151, 156; Northern Ireland Tourist Board, pp. 22, 54, 76, 83, 97, 117, 168, 170, 172, 174, 177; Richard Sealy, p. 180; Shannon Free Airport, pp. 2–3, 30, 71, 73, 81, 86, 136, 169, 182, 192, 195, 200, 201, 203; Studio M, jacket photo and pp. 68, 79, 93, 199, 206, 207; United Press International, p. 179. Permission is gratefully acknowledged.

Copyright © 1970 by Arnold Dobrin

All rights reserved under International and Pan-American Conventions. Published in Camden, New Jersey, by Thomas Nelson Inc. and simultaneously in Don Mills, Ontario, by Thomas Nelson & Sons (Canada) Limited.

First edition

Library of Congress Catalog Card Number: 70–117146

Manufactured in the United States of America

j 941.5
D634i

Acknowledgments

For their cooperation and kindness the author is deeply grateful to Mr. Bill Maxwell of the Irish International Airlines, Sean White of the Irish Tourist Board, Vi O'Sullivan, Norah Niland, Petronella O'Flanagan, Tom Sheehy, Dr. and Mrs. Andrew Ganly, Kathleen Comyn, Peter and Helena Brennan, Michael J. Healy, J. P. Murray, and Joan Ennis. There are many more whose names should appear here; when one is writing of Ireland, such a list is sure to be a long one.

Books by Arnold Dobrin

Aaron Copland: His Life and Times
Igor Stravinsky: His Life and Times
Italy: Modern Renaissance

NORTH CHANNEL

• LONDONDERRY

ULSTER

BELFAST

NORTHERN IRELAND

CONNACHT

IRISH SEA

ATLANTIC OCEAN

GALWAY •

DUBLIN ●

LEINSTER

SHANNON AIRPORT

KILKENNY •

LIMERICK

MUNSTER

WATERFORD

CORK •

IRELAND

Contents

Slea Head Beach in County Kerry on the west coast

An Island People

All the countries of Europe are different from each other in a great many ways, but there is something very special about the way Ireland differs from the rest of the continent. This is the subject of a vast number of books and articles that attempt to analyze this unusual island and its people. But as the peculiarities of the weather, the character of the land, and the stormy political past are discussed, the reader (especially if he is about to be a visitor to Ireland and is impatient to be off) soon finds his head swimming. The historical facts, the fantasies, conjecture, and contradictions create only more confusion in his mind—so much confusion that finally only the simple images remain: images of a simple country people, of adamant Catholicism, of wet weather and of greenery.

You may have heard of this legendary greenery all your life, and you may be bored by the advertisements that focus on it and the endless clichés that revolve around it. And yet it is the greenness—the lush green fields of Ireland—that catch your attention as soon as you arrive.

Some parts of the island are greener than others, but, taken as a whole, the land is incredibly green—green and moist, for it is the constant moisture in the air that keeps the fields green. As the westernmost edge of Europe, Ireland is cooled—and watered—throughout the year by the Atlantic Ocean's gusts of fresh air, and by the storms that sweep eastward from across the sea.

The weather has a strong influence on the Irish people; the constantly moving clouds, the clear, luminous light, the frequent rainfall—

These young married people own a popular country hotel in Schull, County Kerry

11

all of these seem to contribute to the creation of the unpredictable Irish temperament. The Irish themselves are preoccupied with the changes in the weather; comments on it are an inevitable part of almost every conversation. "Isn't it a grand day—praise be to God!" is a frequently heard accompaniment to the morning's greeting. Or, if it is gray and damp outside, people frequently grumble, *"Desperate* weather we're having!" The Irish writer George Moore used to quote a Mayo farmer's comment that his cottage was damp enough to give rheumatism to a wild duck. Bright, warm days are regarded with great pleasure, and any unusually extended periods of good sunny weather are remembered and discussed long after they have passed.

Other countries on the same latitude as Ireland, such as Labrador, are far colder. The island's temperature remains mild throughout the year because of the warm Gulf Stream, which flows around it; it is the warmth of this water, mixing with the colder air currents, that also creates the unusual moisture.

Generally, the temperature stays between 40 and 60 degrees throughout the year, and there are parts of the southwest coast that are warm enough to produce subtropical growth. Rain falls frequently throughout the year but rarely for long periods. These are not long, hard rains but rather infrequent mists. Snow falls rarely and roses often bloom well into December.

Irish Temperament and Physique

The fairly constant temperature would seem to have a stabilizing effect on the Irish temperament, but just the opposite seems to be true. Although the actual degrees of heat or cold may not fluctuate much, the light, the sun, and wind do. A dark, fierce morning often turns into the gentlest of sunny, warm days by early afternoon. Conversely, a bright, promising day may often result in drenched clothes, drenched spirits, and totally disrupted plans. The constantly changing atmosphere and luminous light are commented upon by every writer who has been to Ireland. Although these are a delight for most visitors, Irish expatriates include them in the list of things that are wrong with Ireland. George

A sunny corner of a cottage at Clogherhead, north of Dublin, is a pleasant place for a neighborly chat

Bernard Shaw, when speaking of the effects of the Irish climate on the people, wrote, ". . . . your wits can thicken in the soft moist air . . ."

The speech of the Irish is as unpredictable as their weather. No one can visit Ireland without being charmed by the fresh and unexpected turn the most ordinary conversation may take. The Irish writer Edna O'Brien writes that one night on a bus she was reading a paper with headlines speculating about what astronauts might find on the dark side of the moon. "An elderly black-shawled woman beside me ran her eyes over the pages and said to me, 'I seen it often in my time.'"

"What?" Miss O'Brien asked.

"The dark side of the moon," said she.

Joe McCarthy reports overhearing two strangers carrying on a conversation in a hotel dining room. One of them, upon leaving, said that it had been a pleasure to talk to his neighbor.

"I would say the same to you, sir," the other man answered, "but it would sound repetitive."

The inventive turn of phrase, the wit, the amusing, succinct observation are an intrinsic part of daily life. Unlike most other countries, in Ireland such witticisms are not confined mainly to the educated classes but are spoken by men from every social and economic level.

The tone of voice in which the Irish speak also adds greatly to their charm. The loud, brash voice is almost unknown in Ireland; people talk softly, some almost in whispers. Their voices are gentle—like the Irish rainfall. The familiar Irish tenor voice is heard everywhere, and the hoarse, rough, or low register with which we associate strong masculinity is exceptionally rare in Ireland.

It is not only the accent but the intonation that is so appealing. The cadence of the Irish voice is catching; it is usually referred to as "lilting," and in spite of the music-hall connotations, that is still a good word to describe it. The nuances, the little rise at the end of a sentence, and many other intangible factors make the speech of the Irish one of the great charms of Ireland.

Ireland is one of the last countries in the world in which conversation remains an art. Country people talk, city people talk; they complain, comment, observe, gossip, whisper. The line between thought and speech seems less acute in the Irish than in other people—perhaps from frequent use. A priest watches an elderly and ailing parishoner hobbling weakly from the church and comments, "He's walking slow but he's going fast." V. S. Pritchett tells of seeing a huge political sign saying "Vote for Duffey" on a wall near Dublin. Next to it the opposition had added, in large letters, "And Ireland's dead will rise to curse you!"

The Irish are far less concerned with time than other people are: Irish clocks are often wrong, and announcements of time over the radio are infrequent. No matter how rushed he may be, the Irishman always has time to stop and talk.

Courtesy is the rule throughout Ireland; salespeople, policemen, bus drivers, and taxi drivers are as courteous as the people you meet socially. The important aspect of the gentlemanly tradition is an old one. It was commented on by the nineteenth-century English writer Thackeray, who wrote in his *Irish Sketch Book,*

> I have met more gentlemen here than in any place I ever saw; gentlemen of high and low ranks, that is to say: men shrewd and delicate of perception, observant of society, entering into the feelings of others, and anxious to set them at ease or to gratify them; of course exaggerating their profession of kindness, and in so far insincere; but the very exaggeration seems to be a proof of a kindly nature, and I wish in England that we were a little more complimentary.

Perhaps the weather has contributed to the development of these Irish characteristics; unquestionably, it has without doubt affected the physical man.

Irish complexions are fresh and ruddy, due mainly, it is thought, to the constant moisture in the air. One Irishman asked about this said that it was the result of giving the milk from only one cow to a child; but since thousands of Irishmen now live in cities—and drink the milk of many cows—this view would seem to be questionable.

Their rural heritage and love of sports have kept a large number of Irishmen lean and hard-muscled; abundant food has also contributed to their physical well-being. According to the most recent United Nations statistics, Ireland is the best-fed nation in the world.

Although the famous dark-haired, dark-eyed Irishman with a very fair skin is common, light-haired types, especially those with auburn or reddish-colored hair, are seen everywhere. Women seem to retain a freshness and radiance beyond youth that most men—unless they live in rural areas—too quickly lose. In his twenties the average city Irishman turns from active participation in sports to becoming an observer; often when he settles into a steady pub-going routine, the physical consequences are inevitable.

It is also during these years that the influence of religion begins to assert itself in a variety of ways. The obsession with sin, the quest

Shooting season runs from November 1 to mid-January. Many of the best preserves are government owned

for purity and religious enlightenment, the repressive measures of dogma—all these pressures begin to show on the face of the average Irishman. In Ireland, religion is a profoundly important influence.

Importance of Religion

Although shops and restaurants in downtown areas tend to open late in the morning, the new visitor to Ireland is sometimes baffled by the heavy foot traffic in certain areas of the city. Upon investigation he will discover that early weekday Masses are important activities for the Irish. Churches are busy places in Ireland; prayers begin early and continue throughout the day (and into the night). Many people on a bus in Dublin make the sign of the cross each time a Catholic church is passed. Roadside shrines with statues of the Virgin are common throughout Ireland, and holy pictures are prominently displayed in Catholic homes. Religion is not only practiced but discussed, written about, and argued over. It is estimated that 95 percent of the Irish people are

Catholics, and of those it is believed that 90 percent attend mass regularly—at least on Sundays.

The population of the Republic of Ireland includes about 150,000 Protestants, but there are quite large areas of the country where non-Catholics are practically nonexistent. (The small Protestant population has been slowly declining since 1870. During the period of the Troubles, there was a very large decline, when a hundred thousand Protestants left the country.) There are approximately 3,000 Jews and in the Republic of Ireland there is little outward bigotry among the different religious groups. The total population of the Republic of Ireland is about 3 million. The much smaller Northern Ireland numbers half that—1.5 million—making a total of 4.5 million Irishmen for both countries. The total area of the island is 32,600 square miles; of which 27,100 square miles belong to the Republic, and 5,500 square miles to Northern Ireland.

The Irish Constitution guarantees religious freedom to all sects and creeds but it has also acknowledged "the special position of the Holy Catholic Apostolic and Roman Church as the guardian of the Faith professed by the great majority of the citizens." There is no separation of church and state, and it is freely acknowledged within the country that the government does not act on any issue without the approval of the Church.

This applies from the highest levels of internal policy to the most minute details of the local village issues. The continuation of this trend is ensured by the strong traditional role that the Church has always taken in public education.

All public elementary education in the country is under religious control; this is true not only of the Catholic Church but also of the Protestant and Jewish religions. The Catholic priest has supervision of the education of all the Catholic children in his parish. He chooses the principal of the school, and his approval is needed for every teacher hired.

Minorities do not suffer any official discrimination. Nuns and priests, who often teach in government schools, receive the same wages as other teachers.

Secondary schools are also supervised by the government. Many high schools and preparatory schools are administered by religious orders.

The clergy are involved not only in the Irishman's education and religious matters but also in most other areas of his life. The priest is consulted for guidance in family or business matters. He resolves problems and squabbles that involve emotional matters, and his opinion is often requested when the selection of the local football team is in question. The special position that the priest has in Irish life can be traced, in part, to the sufferings of past centuries, when the parish priest was the only friend the people had. Little can be accomplished without the priest's approval; his disapproval is an absolute certainty that a plan will fail.

And yet, although the priest is regarded not only as a spiritual leader but as an administrator in temporal matters as well, he rarely has a genuinely intimate relationship with his parishioners. No matter how casual or intimate the relationship may seem, the Irish never forget that the priest's is a very special and very powerful position. The foreigner, having come to Ireland for the first time, may be startled to hear an Irishman say in response to a particular question that the priest will say this or that. The priest's authority is almost always unchallenged.

Even in the smallest rural parishes, the priests are supported mainly by privately paid tithes of a few annual offerings. The practice of passing baskets at Sunday Mass is not practiced. Also, priests in larger parishes are given rectories to live in by themselves. Curates are also given houses.

The characters and temperaments of the important members of the clergy are known and discussed throughout the country; they are important public personages and their public appearances and ecclesiastical ceremonies are given coverage in the press.

There are few cooperative efforts between Catholic and Protestant priests in Ireland. Every aspect of life, whether it is economic, social, or educational, is affected by the great division between Catholics and Protestants. Each group reads its own newspapers, patronizes banks and shops that are owned by persons of the same faith, and joins separate

Parish priest enjoying the music at a festival in Tipperary

athletic teams. There are even separate Protestant and Catholic Boy Scout organizations.

An Irishman, upon making the acquaintance of a new person, will not know how to proceed with a continuing relationship until he has discovered the other's religion. Except in rare instances, the fact that the newcomer is of a different religion can determine that there will never be a close bond between the two.

Marriages between Catholics and Protestants are rare in Ireland, and those who insist upon such a union are subjected to severe discrimination and social pressures from both communities.

The Irish believe themselves to be a spiritual nation; indeed, there are times when the sin of pride in spirituality is all too clear. And yet it is true that a definite tendency toward monasticism has been noted almost since Irish history began to be recorded; however, part of the severity of Irish Catholicism can be traced to French influence.

Toward the end of the eighteenth century, the British government (which then treated Ireland as a colony) became increasingly disturbed by the rising tide of revolutionary movements in Ireland—especially that led by a Protestant, Theobald Wolfe Tone. In an effort to win the sympathy of the Catholics, they established a new Catholic theological seminary at Maynooth in 1795.

The new seminary was staffed almost entirely by refugees from the French Revolution; they were strict monarchists who deeply detested Tone and his republican ideals. To a man, they respected the divine power of the King and the Pope. These men were influenced by Jansenism, a particularly strict form of Catholicism that was later forbidden by the Vatican. It emphasized severe penances and both intellectual and spiritual chastisements. The Jansenists considered the Jesuits too lenient; these, in turn, found the Jansenists Calvinistic.

Because of the strong influence of the monarchist French Catholic priests at Maynooth, the vast majority of Irish Catholics supported the British against Tone. They favored the 1800 Act of Union, in which

Climbers of Croagh Patrick should always be prepared for rain during the annual pilgrimage

Ireland became part of the United Kingdom, and which was to have such disastrous consequences for all Irishmen.

Some writers believe that the Irish people's interest in physically punishing holy pilgrimages can be traced to the Jansenist influence. Following the theory that going to daily Mass to receive the Sacrament cannot be enough to win salvation, many Irish believe they must scourge themselves by making painful pilgrimages to holy places.

One of the best known of such pilgrimages is the annual ascent of Croagh Patrick, a 2,510-foot mass of rocks overlooking Clew Bay in County Mayo, where Saint Patrick is believed to have fasted for forty days and nights. According to the old legend, it was here that snakes and other reptiles fled from his holiness.

Often more than sixty thousand pilgrims begin that ascent before dawn. Although the chosen time is the last Sunday in July, the weather—this being Ireland—may be cold and rainy. Since many worshipers choose to make their pilgrimages with bare feet, the pain and impairment to their physical well-being at the end of the march can easily be imagined. Most reach the summit with feet that are bloodied and bruised. Along the way, the faithful make many stops to pray, and when they have finally reached the summit, the sun has begun to rise. Then all kneel to attend Mass.

There are many other pilgrimages as well as that to Croagh Patrick. Another popular pilgrimage is to Lough Derg, a lonely lake in Donegal where, according to tradition, Saint Patrick is believed to have seen a vision of Purgatory. A small basilica dedicated to Saint Patrick is situated on a small island in the middle of the lake; it is here that the faithful, having fasted since the previous midnight, spend the next forty-eight hours in prayer and meditation. No sleep is allowed on the first night; the following day each person is given a piece of dry bread and a cup of black tea during a brief respite from their walk around the basilica without shoes while reciting rosaries and other prayers.

The second night the pilgrims are permitted to sleep in hostels, but when they leave the island on the morning of the third day, they are expected to continue their fast until they reach their homes.

Pony-trekking is a pleasant way to explore County Down, Northern Ireland

Country Pleasures

Many writers have commented at great length on the religious nature of the Irish, on their Catholicism, and on the before-mentioned streak of asceticism that seems to have been present since recorded history. However, there is much evidence that reveals the Irish Catholicism of past centuries to have been quite different than we know it today; what we observe now is Victorian Catholicism. Sin and hell were, apparently, not always so much a part of Irish consciousness; delight in the physical pleasures and joy in nature were a strong part of Irish life. Indeed, their ability to wrest joys from the poorest, humblest moments has enabled the Irish to survive. This characteristic has survived and is a considerable part of Irish charm.

Until the famine, country life in Ireland, for all its hardships, appears to have had many compensations. Without much money or any of the pleasures it can buy, the people made use of their own highly imaginative

22

resources. The custom of visiting one's friends and neighbors was very popular, and witty, gracious, and amusing hosts were much appreciated. Various sports and games were played, but hurling, a game similar to field hockey, was the most popular. Both men and women also liked to sing, tell stories, and to dance—this provided most of the entertainment.

As Victorian restrictions became more severe, the delight in these pleasures faded, but never died. But such restraints left their mark on the Irish character. Centuries of previous English authority and the Catholic hierarchy have also left their imprint; today the Irish are, as Frank O'Connor has put it, "notoriously evasive . . . this vacancy enables the Irishman, like the Spaniard, to muse or reflect on an inner life." A "gift of the gab," an hour's flow of "blarney" allow the Irishman to pass the time without becoming involved or committing himself in any way.

It is this detachment from things which many other peoples have thought essential to progress that once made the Irish seem unrealistic, self-indulgent and not very serious about important matters. Ambitious materialists often find his mental attitude infuriating; they label the Irishman's casual, indolent, speculative nature laziness. He has been thought to be thriftless and unbusinesslike.

There is a half-sad, half-humorous subjectiveness about Irish life which creates a mood of pensive detachment. Perhaps the weather, as we have seen, contributes its share to the strange Irish temperament. Other factors are rooted in the origins of the Irish people.

Early History

In 1928, a cave was found in County Waterford that revealed the existence of two skeletons of the late glacial period. Studies of these bones and other remains (such as flints) are regarded as evidence that men were living in Ireland as early as 6000 B.C. or in what is known to anthropologists as the Upper Palaeolithic period. Presumably, these men preyed on the great Irish elk (now extinct) and reindeer. Although large numbers of flints have been discovered, almost nothing is known of this culture.

It is thought that sometime around 3000 B.C., Neolithic stock raisers and grain growers joined the hunters to form a different kind of society—one more stable and less nomadic. But this point like most other theories referring to this remote period, is a matter still widely disputed among anthropologists.

There is much evidence of the prehistoric past in Ireland. Near Slane Hill in County Meath, where Saint Patrick lit his paschal fire in 433, there is a Bronze Age burial chamber that is thought to be four thousand years old. This grave is built of great, unhewn stones, some of which are carved with intricate designs. Throughout the country are many stone remnants—all that remains of the prehistoric ring forts, Druid stones, and dolmens, which are burial chambers made of large flat rocks that are balanced on top of upright supporting boulders or slabs. Very little is known of these mysterious rock arrangements, but many authorities believe that they were the altars of ancient sun worshipers, or possibly are sections of tombs that were once covered with earth.

Here, as at Stonehenge in England, the mystery of how these early men could maneuver and haul such huge stones is still unsolved. And invariably they chose hilltops for their burial sites, which vastly increased the difficulties involved in engineering.

Druidic traditions were particularly strong and are believed to have continued long after the people were converted to Christianity. Little is known of the Druid culture, but it appears to have been extremely austere and ascetic, and rigidly controlled by the priests. Many writers believe that these traditions influenced the Irish practice of Christianity and have survived until the present day.

The Druid stone and rock arrangements are just a few of the amazing number of ruins that are seen in the countryside. Medieval castles without roofs, abbeys marked by only two or three walls are found everywhere throughout the island. Most of these were destroyed during times of war, but many thatched cottages, abandoned and falling into decay, have been left deliberately by their owners.

It is these ruins, as well as the moist air, the swiftly scudding clouds, and the swells of fresh sea air blowing over the land, which combine to create the moody atmosphere of Ireland that some writers have called

This prehistoric stone circle in County Kerry is called Druid's Castle. In the background is the town of Kenmare

despair. The softly falling rain nourishes the grass growing in the cracks of the stones or in the thatches of the roofs that remain. The timbers are rotten, the floors have turned to grass, and the sky is the roof. Picking your way through the ruins, you remember that people once lived and worked here; that they were warm and protected from the elements in the small whitewashed rooms; that then life became too difficult and they emigrated to a foreign land. But to emigrate has become possible only in fairly recent times. For centuries there was no choice but to stay and struggle and endure. Ireland's conquerors came early and stayed long.

The earliest rulers were the Gaelic Celts—a race of fair-haired, tall men who may have come to the island as early as 350 B.C. With their superior weapons of iron they were able to defeat the inhabitants who already lived there, survivors of an earlier age who did not know how to make iron and had only the weaker bronze weapons with which to defend themselves.

Not much is known of the Celts. Plato in the *Laws* wrote of them as a people who were inclined to drunkenness and a love of fighting. One of the greatest of the Celtic kings was Niall of the Nine Hostages, who ruled at Tara, legendary seat of the Irish high kings, from A.D. 379 to 405. (His direct descendants, the O'Neills of Tyrone, were the Earls of Ulster until 1603.)

Niall disliked peace and was constantly planning and making raids on Britain and, according to some legends, the coast of Normandy. On one of his expeditions abroad he found and brought back a young Roman boy called Patrick, who had been living with his family—Latin-speaking Christians in Britain, which was then just an outpost of the far-flung Roman Empire.

Streets in Dublin are lined with viewers of the annual Saint Patrick's Day parade on March 17

Patrick was sold as a slave and spent many years of his young life herding sheep on the mountains of County Antrim. Eventually he escaped to the continent, studied for the priesthood, and finally returned to Ireland in A.D. 432 as a bishop, fired with the determination to bring Christianity to the barbarians with whom he had spent his youth.

To Patrick, the native Irish must have seemed very savage indeed. He had studied in monastic centers that were previously colonies of the Roman Empire. The Empire itself had disintegrated, but the civilization it had represented was still in evidence.

This was not the case in Ireland, where the Romans had never set foot. While large parts of Europe were familiar with the impressive Roman architecture, with its laws, literature, theater, and the tradition of the bath, the inhabitants of Ireland were living in a most primitive state.

Patrick had grown up in a society that rejected the pagan religion of Rome. The people had forgotten most of the Empire's splendors, but they were still the product of its civilizing influence. Although statues of the Roman gods might be mutilated, most of the great aqueducts and amphitheaters survived in good condition. By the fifth century, many Roman temples had been destroyed, but others had become churches. This was the background of young Patrick's life; possibly he was one of the first Europeans to discover how remote Ireland was from the intellectual and cultural developments on the continent, that Ireland was not only geographically the edge of Europe.

Returning to the island, Patrick brought Christianity to a people who did not have the advantages of the cultural refinements that much of Europe had known for centuries; the mysticism and ritual of Catholicism had enormous appeal to the native Irish. With the knowledge of Latin Patrick brought them, they were able to follow the prayers and gospels. The conversion of an entire people made rapid progress.

Since that time, Catholicism has profoundly affected every aspect of Irish life. The Catholic influence in the government can be understood after reading these first words of the Constitution that was adopted in July, 1937.

> In the name of the Most Holy Trinity, from Whom is all authority and to Whom, as our final end, all actions both of men and States must be referred . . . We, the people of Eire, do hereby adopt, enact, and give to ourselves this Constitution.

Political Life

The Constitution declares Ireland to be a sovereign, independent, and democratic state. The form of government is democratic and is similar to that of the United States. The chief of the Executive Branch is the President, who is elected by the direct vote of the people. He holds office for seven years and is eligible for reelection only once.

Parliament consists of the President of Ireland and two Houses; the House of Representatives (Dáil Éireann) and the Senate (Seanad Éireann). The 144 members of the Dáil are elected by voters on the system of proportional representation. The maximum term is seven years.

The Seanad is composed of 60 members of whom 11 are nominated by the Taoiseach (Prime Minister), and 49 are elected; 3 by the University of Dublin, 3 by the National University of Ireland, and 43 are chosen by five panels of distinguished persons who are experts in such fields as literature, art, education, labor, industry, commerce, public administration, and social services.

The President appoints 7 to 15 members who constitute the government. These men are responsible to the Dáil. They follow the leadership of the Prime Minister, who is appointed by the President from a group of names submitted by the Dáil. The Prime Minister carries far more responsibilities than the President.

The President, as titular head of the government (on the advice of the Prime Minister), summons and dismisses Parliament; he signs and makes public the laws.

The Senate amends legislation but has no veto power. Although it has the power to delay bills passed by the Dáil for a maximum of ninety days, and also to recommend changes, it cannot block the bill permanently.

The average Irishman may not *act* on the viewpoint he expresses, but

A Dublin City Councilor, wearing his official robe and war decorations, attends the Saint Patrick's Day parade

he is sure to have an opinion on the activities of the government. Perhaps more than most men, he is interested in and aware of political life.

Since one of the enduring interests of the Irish is politics, it follows naturally that Irishmen also make good politicians. The weeks previous to an election are particularly exciting times in Ireland; the percentage of people who turn out to vote is said to be one of the highest in any democratic country.

It is possible to visit the Dáil in Dublin and have a sampling of Irish political oratory; but the visitor should first be forewarned that all too often the interchanges will not be very different from those in the parliaments of many other countries.

And yet, despite the unusual interest in political matters, there are few civic groups that have influence on either local or national levels. The average man seems to regard the political arena as something

29

A tinker family. Tinkers are a colorful sight in Irish towns and villages. Their wagon is probably the only "home" these tinker children have

removed from the power he has as a citizen and voter. As in so many other areas of Irish life, the large degree of genuine freedom to choose is not exercised by the average man; instead, he rather humbly accepts the decision of authority.

Not long ago in a series called "The Young Idea," which appeared in the Irish press, Mary Kenny, an Irish student in Paris, wrote,

> In going to school in Paris I was obliged to learn the Rights of Man off by heart; in drinking coffee in cafes I heard waiters and workers and artisans talking about *la liberté*. The great revelation that comes over so many of our exiles hit me slowly but with force. I discovered the meaning of individual rights, the meaning of criticism, the meaning of the civil state of man.

Ireland's small size makes it easy for everyone to know what is happening within the country; this pertains even to the use of the telephone, for there is only one phone book in Ireland. You needn't know where someone lives to find him—you have only to look up his name, which is, of course, listed alphabetically. And yet, in spite of its small size and the cohesiveness of Irish life, there is, paradoxically, a feeling of great space in Ireland. It is possible to drive for many miles along an Irish road without passing anyone; when you do, it may be one of those absurdly romantic tinker's wagons that seem to be directly from the pages of a child's picture book.

Tinkers

One of the most colorful sights of the Irish roads are the wagons of the tinkers and, if they are stationary, the evidence of tinker life surrounding them. Part of this may be a goat or two, usually a few horses, hedges spread with tinker clothes that are drying—and an abundance of dirty but healthy and often beautiful children.

The life of the tinkers is nomadic, and although it resembles the life of the gypsies in other ways, the tinkers are not gypsies and do not speak Romany. However, like gypsies throughout the world, tinkers do metalwork and trade in horses. They also camp by the roadside wherever they please and do not mind lifting a chicken or two from a nearby farm. They tell fortunes, beg in the cities, and are a prominent feature at horse fairs and market days. And although its effectiveness may be open to question, the beauty of an Irish tinker woman's blessing is not. Often you may hear the Tinker prayer asking that ". . . every hair on your head might turn into a candle to light your way to heaven," or "May God and his holy mother take the harm of the year away from you."

It is on the roads, among the tinkers, and in the far west that you may hear Ireland referred to as Eire—the Gaelic (or Irish) name for Ireland. (It is pronounced to rhyme not with "fire" but with "fairer.")

Less colorful than the tinkers, the Anglo-Irish are another small cohesive group of people who have had a profound influence on Irish history.

The Anglo-Irish

Although the Anglo-Irish comprise only 5 percent of the population of the Republic, these families—descendants of the English "planters"—are an important part of the Irish scene. And while these men were, and still are, planters in a literal sense—the owners of large plantations—there is an important connotation the word carries. These Englishmen were sent to Ireland in the hope that they would transplant English culture, laws, and traditions. As they developed—or so the English government reasoned—the Irish sense of identity would gradually die.

At one time the planters were called "the gentry"; although the name has now gone out of fashion, their habits, wealth, and attitudes have remained much the same as they were throughout past centuries.

The Anglo-Irishman usually owns an estate in the country, where he does a good deal of riding and fox hunting. He wears well-cut tweeds,

Muckross House, once part of a vast private estate, is now a National Park in the beautiful Killarney lake district

speaks with an English accent, and is more international in his outlook than other Irishmen. In fact, to many a visitor who has a preconceived idea of Irish characteristics, he seems to be far more English than Irish.

During the years of English rule, the Anglo-Irish (basically of Protestant stock, with some native Irish blood and also a little French Huguenot) were an elite group who have been accused of draining the country of its wealth; the far more numerous Catholic Irish were in many cases no more than serfs. And yet, after centuries of living in the country, the Anglo-Irish saw themselves as true Irishmen. William and Constance Kehoe write, "For centuries the Anglo-Irish have lived in a strange kind of halfway-house, finding themselves 'Irish to the English and English to the Irish.' A double identity is implicit in the very name; they are Irish, but with a difference."

This group has made enormous contributions to the country intellectually, culturally, and politically. Many of Ireland's most valiant fighters in her struggle for independence have come from this group. Yeats and his followers, who worked to restore Ireland's cultural riches, were also a part of it. Although the Anglo-Irish influence is somewhat diminished today, it is still a significant force in Irish life.

The descendants of the Anglo-Irish are very English in their behavior; the visitor to Ireland will find it difficult to see in them any resemblance to the unfortunate image of the "stage Irishman" that the world associates with Ireland.

The Stage Irishman

A visit to Ireland of any length is certain to have one effect: it will destroy the visitor's image of the stage Irishman—the boisterous, dancing, drinking, lazy, fighting figure that many people throughout the world mistakenly think of as the typical Irishman. In Ireland people are especially sensitive about this distorted image, and it is quickly apparent, in conversation with the men of the Irish Tourist Board, that elimination of this false idea is one of their most important objectives.

Such figures do exist, of course, and one of the more notable examples in recent years was the late writer Brendan Behan. What the casual and

Brendan Behan. He wrote a play about his own life, Borstal Boy, *which was banned in Ireland*

uninformed observer fails to understand is that such men are often deliberately playing a part. They realize their audience (whether it is a true audience or just a group of people in a bar) expect a certain kind of behavior from them; because he wishes to please, because he may even enjoy the role for a time, because he wants everyone to have a pleasant evening, he acts as he is expected to act. Perhaps most often his true feelings—like those of another supposedly amusing and romantic figure, the stage Italian—are deeply hidden.

Often people who visit Ireland go there expecting to find prime examples of the stage Irishman. They expect a verbal spectacle studded with wit and fascinating stories. It frequently happens, they discover with surprise, that their overtures toward instant friendship are not ways successful.

The Irishman will never be curt, rude, or abrupt, but he may easily remain at a gracious distance. He is often shy—and this is particularly true of country people. Still, when approached in the right manner, he becomes a friendly conversational partner more easily than almost any other European. Certainly he is one of the most discussed and written about.

The Edge of Europe

There is something unforgettable about approaching an Irish village late in the afternoon after a storm has passed. The steeple of a stone church rises in the clear light above the whitewashed cottages. The surrounding fields are sharply, intensely green, crossed by the dark shadows of swiftly moving clouds and shafts of clear, bright sunlight. Toward evening, white mists rise from the hollows, becoming heaviest near the streams, ponds, and rivers. The hills turn blue and the only sound is that of the wind blowing through the long fresh grass and the splash of water on stones as the clear cold streams rush seaward.

This is the hour when you can smell the scent of turf fires and see puffs of blue peat smoke coming from the cottage chimneys. After dinner, the local pub will be the only place to go and, should you be thinking of spending the night in the village, it is unlikely that you will be able to. The country inn—an inevitable fixture of English village life—is absent in Ireland.

You will have to drive on in the gathering darkness to the next town. The atmosphere is one of greenness and moisture—a moisture that not only keeps the fields green and lush but encourages the extraordinary growth of ivy, lichens, and mosses so characteristic of the Irish roadside. They grow from a soil that is, for the most part, fertile and rich— particularly in the river valleys.

But there are also a large number of bogs throughout the country;

A thatch-roofed Kerry cottage with a freshly dug pile of peat drying nearby

Kenmare, on the southwest coast, is warm enough for palms and other exotic plants to flourish

in many areas, poor drainage and heavy rainfall combine to create widespread boglike and marshy conditions. And although many thousands of acres of valuable land cannot be planted or used for pasture, they still serve a very important function. As the decaying vegetable matter builds up in the marshy areas, it creates a substance called peat. When this is well dried, it is—and has been for centuries—the principal source of fuel for the Irish people. Because it is so cheap and readily available, the Irish, even in times of great hardship, have never been forced to endure the cold known so well to millions of continental Europeans.

However, even with her large deposits of peat, Ireland would still suffer from severely cold winters were it not for the warm waters of the Gulf Stream that surround the island. The fact that Ireland is an island on the outer edge of Europe is often brought into account for much of its history and even the temperament of its people.

The Emerald Isle

Ireland is about 170 miles wide and 300 miles long; the country is approximately the same size as Austria, or the state of Maine.

Although there is a good deal of variety in the Irish landscape, the extreme contrasts found in many other countries do not exist. Most of the coastline is rugged, with rocky shores and cliffs that plunge vertically into the sea below. And although sandy beaches are not common, there are more than enough to please sun and water lovers—both for the Irish and their visitors. You are never more than sixty miles from the sea in any part of Ireland.

The eastern and southern parts of the country are intensely green and often wildly beautiful, with superb meadows or rolling country. A few areas of the southwest are able to boast the growth of subtropical plants. The center of the island is a great plain made partly of limestone pasture land and partly peat bog. Although the Irish call the hills, which rise in many parts of the land, "mountains," for anyone who has lived near the Alps, Dolomites, or the American Rockies, the name is misnomer, for the highest is not much over three thousand feet. This is Carrantuohill, 3,414 feet high.

The west and northeast are the poorest parts of the country; trees are rare, and the land is for the most part stony and barren. Here the coast, although dramatically beautiful, is barren and windswept. This is the

An Aran Islander is bringing home the kelp. O'Brien's Castle can be seen in the background

39

land of the thatched-roof cottage, the primitive donkey cart, and old women dressed in long black shawls. Here, too, are found most of the people who continue to speak Irish (or Gaelic).

On the primitive Aran Islands just off the western coast of Ireland, the people lead an extremely simple life, one of the harshest that any of the Irish have had to endure. Many of the islanders stills weave the wool for their clothing.

The fact that the Aran Islands are thirty miles from Ireland has profoundly altered their way of life; in a similar way, Ireland's separation from England has influenced her own history. Geologists believe that in prehistoric times a land bridge connected the two islands. When this bridge was destroyed, many plants and animals that developed in Britain had no way of reaching Ireland; consequently, there are only two thirds as many varieties of plants in Ireland as there are in Britain.

Ireland has relatively few land mammals. The Irish hare, otter, fox, and badger are abundant, but a great many of the animals that are

A sheepherder and his dog move the flock to new pasture in County Wicklow. Drivers in rural Ireland must look out for cattle on the roads

common in Britain are not found in Ireland. There are only two varieties of mice and—as is generally known—no snakes. They were, according to legend, driven from the island by Saint Patrick.

At one time, the land was heavily wooded, but there are now no forests. This has been pasture land for centuries; for almost twelve months of the year it is covered with the lush green grass that is perfect grazing land for the country's large herds of cattle. It is this grass—indigenous and self-renewing—that has proved the country's greatest capital asset. Because of it, Ireland has been able to build not only her bloodstock and cattle industries, but also the increasingly important dairy industry.

Ireland covers 31,840 square miles (26,602 in the Republic of Ireland). Some of the land is mountainous and much of it is given over to extensive bogs and marshes.

When the peat is brought in from the bog, it is not fit for use. Often it is exposed to the air so that it can dry. It is a brown, spongy substance, composed of plant fibers broken down by the effects of the water and wind over the centuries into something that is a cross between a sod of clay and a chunk of tree bark. It doesn't look as though it would burn. It does not project a strong heat, but it does smolder away even if it sometimes does not catch fire, and it has a very pleasant aroma.

There are two distinct types of turf or peat in Ireland. One marks the site of long-vanished lakes and is mainly composed of the rotted remains of the reeds and other plants that once grew in the area. The other type, was formed by the effect of the heavy moisture of the atmosphere on the moss and lichens that are so abundant in the western areas of the country. It is known as a blanket bog and can be seen sprawling across the uplands of Donegal and Connemara.

In 1933, the government organized a Turf Development Board, which established a cooperative marketing board to ensure better distribution of turf. Before long, however, it was discovered that the old hand-cut turf was unsuited to commercial exploitation. The board began to study the way such countries as Germany and Russia (which also have large deposits of turf) had been able to successfully develop their own large deposits of turf.

Thirty years ago, the Bog of Allen was a bleak and deserted plain with dark pools of bog water and usually deserted except for the occasional figure of a long turf cutter bent over his spade. The area now is the site of turf-burning power stations that have revitalized whole areas of the midlands, where previously there had been little industry.

For centuries, most of Ireland's industry was confined to the north; this section is still the most heavily industrialized. It was an important factor when a political division was forced upon the country.

Political Division

In 1921, when Ireland won her independence from England, after 750 years of English rule, the country was divided into two parts. From the twenty-six countries the Irish Free State was established as a British dominion. However, the six countries in the northeast section of the island, long known by the ancient name of Ulster, were now called Northern Ireland; they remained in the United Kingdom.

A new Constitution in 1937 changed the name of the Irish Free State to Eire. But in 1949, the twenty-six countries seceded from the British Commonwealth, and the Republic of Ireland was formed.

The Republic of Ireland, with which most of this book is concerned, is comprised of the three provinces of Munster, Leinster, and Connaught; these are divided into twenty-six counties, including Donegal in the northwestern part of the island. Although it is a part of Ulster, because of its large Catholic population and other cultural ties with the south, Donegal did not become part of Northern Ireland at the time of the separation but remained attached to the Republic.

Ireland is a rural country; until recently, as many as 60 percent of her population lived on farms. Even Irish towns are often thought to have a rural quality about them. However, this does not apply to Dublin, the capital.

A Spacious Georgian City

Dublin has a unique charm that is recognized by most visitors who have the chance to explore it. For the most part, it is Georgian and early Victorian in character. Compared to the other capitals of Europe, the

42

The River Liffey flows through the heart of Dublin

city is small—slightly more than half a million inhabitants—but it has a bustling nature that makes all the other cities of Ireland unmistakably provincial. Like Paris, its prestige and prominence in commerce and the arts overshadow all the other towns in the land.

Dublin Bay and the safety it provided made an ideal shelter for the early invaders of Ireland. Another feature of its geography is the gentle River Liffey, which afforded an easy route to the rich Irish midlands. Consequently, this was one of the first sites colonized by the invaders. The name Dublin (*Dubh Linn*), or Dark Pool, refers to the dark bog waters of the Liffey.

Much of Dublin was designed in the eighteenth century by men who realized they had a good deal of space to use and used it wisely. It is that very sense of spaciousness and airiness that continues to give Dublin much of its appeal. For this the Irish, and those who have grown to love Dublin, can thank a special commission—"For Making Wide and

Four Courts on the Liffey in Dublin is an impressive Georgian building. It houses the Irish Law Courts

Convenient Streets"—which was set up by the government in the mid-eighteenth century.

The men who created this commission—and dominated the life of Dublin during this period—were the Anglo-Irish; they had wealth, taste, and a desire for elegance. They could afford to employ the best craftsmen and architects to build and furnish new homes for themselves. All of the beautiful Georgian houses on St. Stephen's Green, on Merrion and Fitzwilliam Squares (which are for the most part now occupied by business and government agencies) were built by the Anglo-Irish.

These foresighted men are also responsible for having created the largest park in Europe—the Phoenix Park. This name has nothing to do with the legendary bird but is a corruption of the Gaelic name for a nearby spring, the Fionn-Uisge. The park itself was intended as a deer park and today you can still see the descendants of the original English deer nibbling fresh young leaves from its trees.

Dublin is not an industrial city. It has always been the center of administration and government; for hundreds of years it was a viceregal court. Because of the absence of factories, there is no smog; the wind, always damp and fresh, has a gentle quality.

This unpolluted air has been good to the bricks of which Dublin is built, in a great range of colors from pink and raw crimson to brown and

Along the Grand Canal one can still find some of Dublin's fine Georgian houses

speckled cadmium. These bricks contrast beautifully with the white woodwork seen everywhere—it trims the tall Georgian windows, the pilastered doorways, the fine fanlights of many buildings. Many Dubliners are now concerned about the preservation of this Georgian charm, which is being threatened by the redevelopment that is rapidly changing much of Dublin. But often new flats replace tenements that were among the worst in Europe.

From O'Connell Bridge you can see some of Dublin's new skyscraper buildings, one of which marks the site of the old Liberty Hall, a trade-union headquarters from which the main body of rebel troops marched out on that famous Easter morning more than fifty years ago to take over the General Post Office and declare Ireland a republic.

The pace of Dublin is unhurried, and its leisurely quality is a characteristic that makes it especially attractive to harried visitors from abroad. At first the disordered frenetic traffic would seem to contradict this, but fortunately, the hectic congestion is confined to the traffic. The Irish people have remained easygoing, and they are not dominated by the clock.

One feels comfortable in Dublin; the city is neither brash, nor quaint, nor grand. For the most part, it is flat, but the suburbs to the south are hilly, rising toward the Wicklow Mountains. Here are some of Dublin's most charming houses, with terraces and gardens, and miles of good beaches. In some of the sunny inland hollows, the vegetation is almost subtropical. In this area, just about a forty-five-minute drive from the heart of Dublin, is the Martello Tower, which was once used by James Joyce as a study and is today a small Joyce museum.

"The Rebel City"

Cork is Ireland's second city. The name in Irish is Chorcaigh, which means marsh or swamp and refers to the land surrounding the River Lee (flowing through the center of the city), which at one time was very marshy. Today the city sprawls over the surrounding hills and is one of the most charming cities of Ireland. Along the quays still stand the beautiful old eighteenth-century houses where the rich merchants once lived, but today they have become warehouses and places of business.

46

Cork originally grew up around the monastic school founded by Saint Finbarr in the early seventh century. It then passed into the hands of the conquering Norsemen and later was conquered by the Anglo-Normans. In Ireland, Cork is sometimes called "the rebel city" because of the important part it has played in all national uprisings. The main business district, the city hall, and the public library were burned in 1920 by British constabulary troops. Consequently, resentment against the partition has remained strong in this area.

Cork's unique charm is mainly based on its natural features. It is almost impossible not to be delighted by its many bridges, its hilly streets, and the presence of the beautiful River Lee. Because of its position at the head of Cork Harbour, the city has a considerable amount of commerce. The quays can handle the largest vessels and the harbor is often a scene of bustling activity. One thing is certain: as Ireland's economy grows, so the city of Cork will grow.

Government Ownership and Private Enterprise

Economically, Ireland is one of the most highly socialized countries in Western Europe. State-owned companies employ a third of all industrial workers and produce a third of all manufactured goods. One of the giant state combines, similar in structure to many of the great Italian government-owned combines, is Cora Iompair Eireann (C.I.E.), which is in the sea transport, rail, canal, road, and hotel business. The Irish Peat Development Board, The Irish National Stud, Irish International Airlines are only a few of the other government-owned companies.

The involvement of the Catholic Church in business is of course shrouded in mystery, but it is to be presumed that in Ireland, as in socialist Italy, the Church is actively engaged in many behind-the-scenes business enterprises.

The curious thing is that unlike the socialist countries of Eastern Europe, the atmosphere of the country is strictly a free-enterprise one.

Many large businesses are still privately owned, of course, and one of the most famous is the Guinness Brewery, which is one of the largest in

A "jarvey." Once a popular form of transport, these carriages are now used by the Guinness Brewery as a tourist attraction

Europe. It is a unique organization that has always set the pace for social benefits and wage levels in the business community. Although in operation for over two hundred years, it has never been struck. The Guinness social conscience has benefited not only its workers but also the general social and cultural life of the entire country. Today it is the country's largest private employer, its largest industrial exporter, its largest private taxpayer.

Meat on Friday

Ireland's deeply indented western coastline has many natural harbors, and its continental shelf extends for more than two hundred miles out into the Atlantic—two reasons for the excellent conditions for a prosperous fishing industry. And yet, in all of Ireland, there are only 1,600 full-time and about 4,000 part-time fishermen. Less than 10 percent of the fish caught in Irish coastal waters is landed by Irishmen in Irish vessels.

Fishermen tend their lobster traps at Inishbofin Island off the coast of Galway

What makes this situation even more incredible is the curious fact that Ireland yearly imports quantities of fish meal, which she must have as a fertilizer. No one is exactly sure of why the Irish do not like to fish, including the government, which is trying to find out more about it through studies recently begun by the Irish Sea Fisheries Board.

Thousands of Irishmen of all ages and walks of life were asked why they didn't eat fish except on Friday, the traditional day of abstinence for Irish Catholics. A frequent answer was that they did not want to eat fish on other days because they were forced to do so on Friday. Apparently, this dietary law, which had been enforced so many centuries, accounted for the feeling that the eating of fish was a kind of penance. Even when the restrictions against the eating of meat on Friday were lifted, the Irish aversion for fish continued.

The prejudice against the eating of shellfish is particularly strong in the southwest. Some observers believe this is a holdover from the days of the famine, when people were forced to subsist on whatever shellfish could be gathered from their rocky shoreline.

Apparently, at that time the idea grew in the people's minds that shellfish (and finfish as well) was the food of the poor and must be eaten only when no other alternative was possible.

Another theory, which is less valid, is that fish is more difficult to cook than meat. Cooking has never been regarded as an art in Ireland, a fact that has led an amazing number of writers to critical observations on the average housewife's ability to prepare good food.

And yet none of these theories satisfactorily explain the Irish distaste for fish, or why the people have not taken advantage of their excellent geographical position to create a strong fishing industry. Their aversion is an ancient one, far older than the famine years. It dates back as far as the reign of Charles I, when the Dutch were granted licenses to fish in Irish waters, followed, in the seventeenth century, by others, such as Swedes.

Many observers of the Irish scene feel strongly that the fisherman is not an appealing figure to the average Irishman. His work is viewed as a wet, dangerous, and unattractive job, which should be avoided if at all possible. Even the commercial fisherman prefers not to be at sea overnight. Generally he will set out early in the morning, five days a week, and return in the evening.

Now serious efforts are being made to change these old patterns. Ireland currently exports fish to twenty-two countries. Although the revenue brought in is not very much, it is gradually increasing, and the Sea Fisheries Board hopes to see a steady rise in the fish harvest—and the income from fish sales.

Centuries of Subjection

The year A.D. 795 is a memorable date in Irish history. As the year of the first Viking invasion, it definitely marked the end of one period and the beginning of another, and though it concluded what many writers consider Ireland's golden era, it also brought an infusion of new blood, new ideas, and commerce into the country.

Prior to this date, the Irish had been used only to fighting relatively minor skirmishes among themselves. Numerous chieftains ruled their own, jealously guarded, territories; occasionally one strong enough to dominate most of the others became the "high king." In weaponry and fighting skills the various groups were more or less equal, and none of the tribes were a match for the huge blond, well-trained, and often savage Viking invaders.

The Vikings never missed a chance to plunder, and when they discovered that Ireland's only wealth could be found inside her monasteries, they proceeded to burn and pillage them in their usual manner. The wealth—both of material riches as well as learning—within these centers was prodigious, for Ireland had escaped the horrors of the Dark Ages. During this chaotic time when, on the continent, law and order were almost unknown, Ireland became the refuge for scholars—monks and priests who fled to it for sanctuary. In their trunks they brought rich brocades, vessels of silver and gold, precious stones, illuminated books, and other riches. The Huns and Visigoths never reached Ire-

Ardfert Cathedral, County Kerry. Ruins of ancient monasteries dating from the sixth century dot the map of Ireland

Celtic dancers perform in front of the ancient round tower at Antrim

land; consequently, monastic life and religious scholarship flourished in Ireland as nowhere else in Europe during this period.

Today you cannot tour Ireland without coming across many high, forbidding stone towers, over a hundred feet high, which sometimes are near the ruins of an abbey or may just rise desolately from the plain. It was during the time of the Viking raids that these came to be built as a refuge. The limestone blocks of these towers are cemented together by a very special kind of cement used in the Middle Ages, which, so the legend goes, was made of egg white, cockleshells, animal manure, ox hair, ox blood, lime, riverbed silt, and sand. What the ingredients were no one really knows for certain.

From these watchtowers, the monks would ring bells that warned of the enemy's approach; then people scrambled into the doors, which were fifteen feet above the ground, and tried to find a place of their

own inside. The living conditions in the towers—especially over pro-
longed periods—must have been dreadful. One wonders how many
frozen, hungry, cramped, and frightened men must have mused on the
wisdom of the choice that gave them such a precarious, agonized safety.

The Invaders and the High Kings

The Vikings, whom the Irish called "the light ones" because of their
light hair, were eventually joined by the Danes, who were referred to as
"the dark ones," since they had dark hair. Both groups cleverly chose
the best harbors for their ports. From the nucleus of these tiny ports
grew trading posts, which became the major Irish cities of today.
Dublin, Cork, Waterford, Wexford, and Limerick were all originally
settled by the Norsemen.

This was not accomplished in one or two successful invasions, but by
a long series of raids; as the footholds in the strategic port areas became
more secure, the attacks on the monasteries became more frequent. One
by one these large, rich communities fell before the Norsemen. A
marginal note on a ninth-century manuscript indicates that the monks
lived in almost daily terror. In an apparently spontaneous jotting, one
man wrote:

> Fierce and wild is the wind tonight
> It tosses the tresses of the sea to white,
> On such a night as this I take my ease;
> Fierce Northmen only course the quiet seas . . .

After many years the country was still not overrun; there remained
only bastions of Viking and Danish control. Meanwhile, when not
fighting the invaders, the native Irish chieftains fought with each other.
In 1002, when the legendary Brain Boru became the high king, Irish
resistance stiffened. Boru was not king as we understand the term but
rather a leader of chiefs who more or less controlled the other Irish
chieftains. Under his direction they fought at the Battle of Clontarf in
1014 and broke the power of the Vikings.

It was during this time that all the leading families of Ireland had their names prefixed by *Mac,* meaning son, or *O,* meaning grandson.

The mingling of the Norsemen with the native Irish, which had already begun, now accelerated. They settled down and became part of Irish life. When the Norman kings of England invaded Ireland in the twelfth century, they fought with Irishmen who had now completely integrated with the Norsemen.

The Irish enjoyed about 150 years of self-rule before this Norman invasion from England. (The Normans who ruled England were distantly related to the Vikings. They had crossed the English Channel with William the Conqueror in 1066 to subdue the English.) They are sometimes called the Anglo-Normans or the Welsh Normans, for they were the landless, unsatisfied younger sons of the Norman families that had settled in Wales.

The first wave of Normans ran their ships aground in the south of Ireland at Baginbun, County Wexford, in May of the year 1169. Joining in the assault was an Irishman, Dermot MacMurrough, the powerful King of Leinster, who had been driven from Ireland by Rory O'Connor.

Effigy of a bishop carved in the fourteenth century at Ardfert Cathedral

Celtic crosses in the graveyard of fifteenth-century Muckross Abbey, Killarney

Now Leinster, with his own followers and the Normans, began the domination of Ireland in a way that made the Vikings look like amateurs. Norman destruction and plundering were similar to that of the Vikings, but with an important difference. Being Christians, the Normans believed that their own violent actions were justified because they occurred in defense of their faith. They saw no incongruity between their fierce savagery and their spiritual ideals.

Fear and hatred of the Normans spread among the Irish, who had never seen such armor and well-disciplined bowmen. The Normans were also experts at the arts of battle strategy and siege. Seeing their superior knowledge of warfare, Irish resistance crumbled but did not disappear completely.

When the Normans arrived, they were amazed at the undeveloped conditions of life they found in Ireland. The strong feudal chieftains, whose power was absolute, exploited the Irish peasantry in a manner that horrified even their conquerors. Seán O'Faoláin writes, "The first people to proclaim even an interest in them . . . were the invading English who were shocked at their condition, though to be sure, a political interest urged this human interest."

For a time it seemed that the Normans would merge as completely with the Irish as they had with the Saxons they had found in Britain. The English—who developed from this mixture of the two groups— became a strong cohesive nation and stopped thinking of themselves as either Saxon or Norman. Had this happened in Ireland, almost all authorities are agreed that her history would have been far different from what it in fact became.

The Normans—whom we shall now call the English—ruled with an iron hand; they were the masters of a conquered people, but for the most part they had no wish to integrate. Those who did, formed the great Anglo-Irish families that were to dominate Irish life for centuries; they, too, although coming to think of themselves more and more as Irish, remained apart from the native Irish population.

England's First Colony

The enduring gulf between the two peoples was ensured by the infamous laws passed in the late fourteenth century, which were known as the Statutes of Kilkenny. English leaders, worried about the fact that Englishmen had begun to change their language and their mode of dressing, and appalled at what was considered generally degenerate behavior, decided to act with a firm hand.

The Statutes of Kilkenny, which aimed at keeping the English in Ireland from adopting "the manners, fashion and language of the Irish enemies," became the law for more than two centuries. Their effects were disastrous. They made it illegal for the English to intermarry with the Irish or even to speak the language. If an Englishman was heard speaking Irish, he was liable to be prosecuted or have his land confiscated. Even admitting Irish storytellers or musicians to an English household was considered a crime.

Ireland—England's first colony—endured English oppression; political, economic, and social discrimination made life exceedingly difficult, but, as yet, religious persecution was unknown. It made its appearance when Henry VIII, impatient over delays about the annulment of his marriage to his Spanish queen, Catherine of Aragon, broke away from the Roman Catholic Church. (It was not until 1534-1542 that all of Ireland was brought under English rule. Henry VII was the first English monarch to assume the title of King of Ireland.)

Protestantism spread quickly in England and then among the Anglo-Irish in Ireland. When Henry VIII and his Protestant successors tried to impose this new religion on the Roman Catholic Irish, an intense hatred developed between the two factions, which drastically increased the already high tension prevailing on both sides.

During the Reformation, the Acts of Supremacy and Uniformity were imposed on Ireland by Henry VIII's daughter, Elizabeth I. Queen Elizabeth intensified anti-Irish policy by confiscating Irish lands and giving them to Englishmen. Church properties found ready takers among the land-hungry Anglo-Irish gentry who sought large estates. The saying of Mass was made illegal, and the Irish were forced to contribute support to the newly imposed Anglican clergy—in many cases even where the district had not even one Anglican.

When the Catholic clergy and Catholic schools were outlawed, the priests went underground. Bishops, if discovered, could be hanged, drawn, and quartered. The few priests that remained held secret Masses in the fields while lookouts kept watch for soldiers or informers.

After Elizabeth I was excommunicated by Pius V, anti-English feeling in Ireland intensified and in 1579 finally broke into a major revolt, led by James Fitzgerald (called Fitzmaurice). During this period, seven hundred Italian and Spanish soldiers sent by Pope Gregory XIII and the Catholic Philip II of Spain were massacred by Lord Grey and Lord Ormonde, commanding Queen Elizabeth's colonial troops.

The revolt was completely crushed by the English, who followed it with severe retribution; thousands of the peasantry in the southwest were slaughtered, and still more Irish land was given to the English Protestants. Sir Walter Raleigh was rewarded by a large estate for his efforts to suppress the Irish. It was Raleigh who brought the potato to Ireland from the New World. Queen Elizabeth, who was determined to

*Pilgrim saying the rosary at Knock
Pilgrimage, County Mayo*

put down Irish uprisings with great severity, confiscated 200,000 acres of Catholic-owned land in the southwest of Ireland. As in future years, when confiscations were to become common, the land stolen was always turned over to Englishmen, who, it was hoped, would succeed in eventually anglicizing all of Ireland.

By now Protestantism and England had become closely identified in the Irish mind; Catholicism bound the country to Rome and Spain where, from time to time, she was to turn for aid. Gradually, throughout these difficult years, the ideas of religious fervor and patriotic resistance became one in the mind of the average Irishman.

If it were not for their Catholicism, the Irish would probably have been assimilated into the English nation just as easily as the Welsh and Scots were. But the Irish fought any attempts to be converted to Protestantism, and gradually, as the new religion grew stronger in England, the Catholic Irish were even more drastically cut off from the English. Almost alone among the countries of northern Europe, Ireland remained untouched by the Reformation, just as she had remained untouched by the Renaissance.

"The Degradation of a People"

But there were other reasons besides religion that caused the English to dislike the Irish and the Irish to hate the English. The English knew very well that they were disliked in Ireland, and they knew also that foreign governments were constantly alert to any opportunities to gain a foothold in Ireland, by which they might then, with enthusiastic Irish cooperation, invade England itself. One of the familiar jingles of the day conveyed that fear.

> He that England would win
> Let him in Ireland begin—

Individual Englishmen, however, continued to write enthusiastic reports of the Irish character. Sir Walter Scott reported after a visit, "I never saw a richer country, or, to speak my mind, a finer people; the worst of them is the bitter and envenomed dislike they have to each other. Their factions have been so long envenomed, and they have such narrow ground to do battle in, that they are like people fighting with daggers in a hogshead."

In Ulster, after the defeat of the Irish chief O'Neill, Englishmen and Lowland Scots, mainly of the Presbyterian religion, were "planted." It was the beginning of a tragic history for Ulster (which was to become Northern Ireland after the creation of the Irish Free State). By 1660 the industrious Scots had created a relatively democratic and prosperous community.

Meanwhile, conditions had been worsening in most other parts of Ireland under Oliver Cromwell, whose rule there was perhaps the most savage thus far. By now three quarters of all Irish land was in the possession of the English, a great many of whom were absentee landlords who chose to live grandly in England on their Irish rents. Cromwell was far from indifferent to the economic interests of these men, but he was mainly fired, like many other tyrants, by an intense religious zeal that he believed to justify his cruelties. "I am persuaded," he said, "that this is the righteous judgement of God upon those barbarous wretches who have imbrued their hands in so much blood." After his victory at Drogheda in 1649 (which had become a massacre for the Irish), he declared, "I do not think thirty of the whole escaped with their lives. Those that did are in safe custody for Barbados."

Cromwell continued the hated policy of "plantation," the transplanting of Englishmen throughout the country. Six thousand landowners were still Catholic in 1641, but Cromwell was determined that they should be deprived of their lands. During this period thousands of Irish, including men, women, and children, were sent to work in the Barbados and on the American plantations. Others were forced from their homes and sent to the barren west of Ireland—a fate that was clear enough in the catch-phrase of the time, "Hell—or Connaught!"

After Cromwell's death a period of less intense persecution began. It was to last only until 1695, when the Penal Laws were enacted, which

Statue of Edmund Burke at Trinity College, Dublin

Edmund Burke called "well-fitted for the oppression, impoverishment and degradation of a people, and the debasement in them of human nature itself."

Catholics could not bear arms, vote, or hold office. They were barred from trading and teaching, and could not enter the professions. A Catholic owning a horse worth more than five pounds could have it taken away from him by a Protestant. Children were taught in "hedge schools"—clandestine meetings usually held in the open places that were protected by high shrubbery.

The latter years of the seventeeth century saw still another important triumph for the English. On July 1, 1690, William III won a decisive victory over the Catholic gentry at the Battle of the Boyne and became the undisputed ruler of all Ireland. It was after this battle that the Anglo-Irish aristocracy began to flourish. The English had never had a more secure foothold in Ireland, and they began to pour capital into the country. Throughout the eighteenth century they greatly influenced both town and country life. These aristocrats were responsible for the design of Dublin and for its uniquely graceful atmosphere. The country homes they constructed during this period remain one of the great attractions of Ireland.

Unfortunately, although they derived their wealth from Ireland, most Anglo-Irish families always remained somewhat remote from the native Irish. Intellectuals and artists felt a closer bond with the common people, and it is primarily these to whom Seán O'Faoláin refers when he writes ". . . the new ascendency worked, in selfless devotion in generation after generation, side by side with native Irishmen, to preserve the traditions, language and history of Ireland. These were the men, and they were legion, who were the forerunners of the modern popular Gaelic Revival."

But the arts have always interested men of wealth and leisure. While the Anglo-Irish continued their concern with intellectual and aesthetic matters, the life of the common man in Ireland remained as hopeless and desperate as it had been for centuries.

Throughout the sixteenth, seventeenth, and eighteenth, and much of the nineteenth centuries, the life of the tenant farmer was one of terrible subjection and terrifying poverty. Again, with his wonderful ability to

clearly see and evoke the Irish scene, Seán O'Faoláin writes of these
nameless men,

> They did not prosper. But they held on with a tenacity that is the
> most moving and astonishing spectacle in the whole of Irish story.
> For these centuries, through generation after generation, starving
> not by thousands but by millions, falling into the earth like the
> dung of cattle, weeping and cursing as they slaved, patient alike
> under the indifference of God and their masters, they clung to their
> wretched bits of land with savage fierceness, clung as it were by
> their bleeding fingernails.

In 1798 the Irish rebelled at a time when England was deeply involved
in her struggle with revolutionary France. The Irish, under Theobald
Wolfe Tone, had been assisted with French arms and money, and the
English quelled the rebellion with brutality. Hoping to increase her
domination of Ireland, England then increased her army to a hundred
thousand men. Still more grave events were in Ireland's future.

Union with the United Kingdom

During the last years of the eighteenth century and beginning of the
nineteenth, all the countries of Europe were watchful of the effects
of the French Revolution and later, the rise of Napoleon. Royal governments took all precautions possible to prevent any change in the status
quo and remained alert to any hint of revolution. England, which was
now having enough trouble dealing with Napoleon on the continent, decided that Ireland would be less of a problem if the country officially became a part of Great Britain. Controls could then be more rigidly
enforced, and any attempts by foreign powers to gain a foothold in Ireland might be more quickly destroyed.

The Act of Union, which occurred in January of 1800, was organized in such a way that it seemed a constructive development auguring
well for the Irish people. Irish hopes were raised and spirits high as the
new century began.

Superficially, Ireland appeared to be gaining great advantages. From
this date, free trade would be possible between the two islands, and
the long-standing discrimination against Irish industry would come to a
halt. It also seemed probable that English investors would now direct

capital into Ireland, which was desperately needed for industrial development. It was also suggested by those who appeared to be informed that Catholic emancipation would follow the Act of Union.

But far from creating more favorable circumstances for the Irish, her absorption into the United Kingdom only worsened the serious problems from which she had suffered for so many years. The Act produced a profound change throughout the entire fabric of Irish life.

The Irish Parliament of Dublin was dissolved, and it was assumed that the hundred or so Irish members of the English Parliament at Westminster would ably look after their affairs on the island.

Dublin, instead of being a national capital, now became just another provincial city of England. Most of the Anglo-Irish aristocracy—the men who were responsible for Dublin's eighteenth-century charm and elegance—departed, and the city began a long decline.

Of this period, Frank O'Connor writes eloquently,

> . . . the people were left to their own devices, and their devices were unbelievably inadequate. Since the vast majority of them could not really possess either homes or land, they had lost all their traditional skills. Outside of Ulster they had lost even the two skills without which civilization cannot exist—carpentry and cookery. When they went abroad they could neither build nor cook, so they made bad settlers. There were merely a few million unskilled rustics, speaking a half-dead language they could neither read nor write, thrown in with well-educated populations who were highly skilled in industrial techniques.

Passing years proved that Irish hopes for new opportunities were simply delusions and little else. English capital was not forthcoming. Free trade enabled England to unload surplus goods on the Irish, and Irish industry suffered. Unemployment grew. Even the larger freedoms envisioned by some Irish were not forthcoming; twenty-nine years were to pass before the Catholic Emancipation Act was passed. The man responsible for it was Daniel O'Connell, one of the great heroes of Irish history. He gave up a brilliant career at the bar to devote his life to the emancipation of Ireland.

By 1843, the Irish were seeking a repeal of the Union. These were the bitter, tragic years of the great famine; freedom seemed a hopeless,

Haymaking in County Wicklow

A farmhouse in County Sligo. Ben Bulben, the mountain in the background, inspired some of Yeats's early poetry

futile dream while the struggle for physical survival required every ounce of strength.

Finally, toward the end of the nineteenth century, the almost intolerable burdens the Irish people had had to face began to ease. Formerly, they could be charged any rent their landlord wished to impose, but the Land Act of 1881 stabilized the rents. Another important land act —passed in 1885—provided five million pounds in loans to farmers who wanted to purchase their farms over a period of forty-nine years. Later land acts added another £130 million. Because of these enlightened measures, almost every farmer in Ireland today owns his own bit of land.

The Great Hunger

During the middle of the nineteenth century, Europeans began to travel abroad as they never had before. All who came to Ireland were astonished at the standard of living they found. After seven hundred years of English domination the hopeless poverty of the Irish exceeded that of any other country in Europe. A German traveler named Kohl wrote that no mode of life on the continent could seem pitiable after what he had seen in Ireland. He said that he used to pity the Letts in Livonia. "Well, Heaven pardon my ignorance! Now I have seen Ireland, it seems to me that the poorest among the Letts, the Estonians, the Finlanders, lead a life of comparative comfort."

The Duke of Wellington (who was a native of County Meath) wrote, "There never was a country in which poverty existed to the extent it exists in Ireland."

The only exceptions were to be found in certain parts of Ulster, especially Belfast and its environs, which were rapidly developing into an industrial center that brought wealth to the area. These were the years when the Irish linen trade began to flourish, and soon shipbuilding was to bring in additional wealth.

The records of a census taken in 1836 (in the village of Tullahobagly, County Donegal) show that the nine thousand inhabitants possessed only 10 beds, 93 chairs, and 243 stools. It was not uncommon for the farm animals, such as pigs, to sleep in the same rooms with their

A typical nineteenth-century castle. Such structures are frequently bought by wealthy foreigners, who delight in their reconstruction and decoration

Beehive huts made without mortar were used as dwellings in the monastic period

owners. Manure heaps were piled in front of doorways and sometimes were even found inside the house. People who had been evicted from their homes or were unemployed had to find shelter in the open, and it often happened that they were forced to live in miserable bog holes covered with a makeshift roof of branches or burrowed into banks of earth.

Another census, taken in 1841, graded the inhabitants of Ireland into four economic classes. Those who lived in windowless mud cabins of a single room were consigned to the fourth and lowest class, and these, the census takers were alarmed to discover, constituted nearly half the families of the rural population.

Except for a few men of strong humanist ideals, the landlords were interested only in the money they could extract from their land. Many were absentee landlords—an evil that was noted in Ireland as early as 1377. Only a fraction of the income they received was spent in Ireland.

In 1842 it was estimated that six million pounds gained from Irish rents were spent outside the country. Kohl, the perceptive German traveler, records seeing the mansions of these absentee landlords standing "stately, silent, empty."

Sometimes such landlords visited their estates only once or twice during their lifetimes; some never visited them at all. Consequently, few could feel deeply concerned about the suffering and deprivation that existed generally throughout Ireland or, more particularly, on their own estates. The English philospher John Stuart Mill wrote,

> In Ireland alone the whole agricultural population can be evicted by the mere will of the landlord, either at the expiration of a lease or, in the far more common case of their having no lease, at six months' notice. In Ireland alone, the bulk of a population wholly dependent on the land cannot look forward to a single year's occupation of it.

A fisherman's cottage on the Cashin River

The Potato

And yet, in spite of the great hardships faced by the Irish, the continuation of life was possible because of the relative abundance of one very important food staple—the potato. This food, especially suited to cultivation in small plots of land, made it possible to feed a whole family on a tiny piece of land. To provide the same family with equivalent nourishment in grain would require acreage four to six times as large. Supplementing the potato diet were dairy products, which were fairly easily available in most districts.

The only tool needed for the cultivation of the potato was a primitive spade. Throughout Ireland a method of planting was used called "lazy beds." To grow potatoes by this method, trenches were dug and potato sets laid in the open ground. When the shoots appeared, they were re-earthed again. This type of cultivation was well suited to the moist soil of Ireland; it provided good drainage and allowed the crop to be grown on hilly or rocky mountainsides.

Still another great advantage of the potato was that it was also useful in rearing cattle, pigs, and fowl. These were mostly given tubers too small for human consumption.

One of the disadvantages of the potato was the uncertainty of the crop because of its susceptibility to blight; another problem, almost as serious, was that there was a limit on how long it could be stored. Because of this, nearly 2,500,000 workers who were not regularly employed frequently went hungry during the summer months, when nothing was left of the old potato crop and the new one was not yet harvested. June, July, and August were for this reason popularly called the "meal months"—that unfortunate period when people were forced to buy grain in order to survive until the next potato harvest.

Living with Poverty

The potato had considerable influence on the social life of the Irish. Since it required much less time and effort to produce than any other staple food, the peasantry had more time for leisure than similar groups in other countries.

In this cottage, near Shannon Airport, only the sewing machine is relatively modern, but it is hand operated

Especially during the long winter nights the people loved to sit in their warm cabins talking for many hours, telling stories and often dancing, as well. Their fuel, peat cut from nearby bogs, cost little or nothing. There was always a good deal of it, so that heat was never a serious problem for even the poorest. The relatively easy accessibility of both food and fuel gave the Irish time for leisure and reflection that no other agricultural people knew.

In warmer weather it had been the custom for centuries to gather at the crossroads and dance through the dusk into the night. A wake (the watch that is held over a dead body prior to burial) was a great social occasion, a time for pleasure and a good deal of drinking. George

Nicholls, a visiting Englishman, wrote, "If there be a market to attend, a fair or a funeral, a horse race, a fight or a wedding, all else is neglected and forgotten."

Many travelers have commented on the consistent courtesy, the good manners, and the hospitality of the Irish of all classes, no matter what their economic level. Sir Walter Scott notes the ". . . perpetual kindness in the Irish cabin; buttermilk, potatoes, a stool is offered, or a stone is rolled that your honor may sit down . . . and those that beg everywhere else seem desirous to exercise hospitality in their own houses."

An English girl, Elizabeth Ham, wrote that she was amazed to find that in Ireland, unlike England, she could roam the woods and fields alone without any fear of being molested. She wrote she would have "fearlessly trusted the Irish peasantry in any circumstances."

Many times this Irish hospitality and courtesy stemmed from old memories of faded grandeur that had been handed on through the generations. It is said that the Irish beggar—who claimed to be descended from kings and was consequently a figure of fun in Victorian days—was in fact a man who came of an aristocratic lineage. Until the famine, many poor peasants in mud cabins made wills bequeathing the estates that had long ago been confiscated from their forefathers.

And yet, although the Irish had learned to live with their poverty, mere survival continued to require an enormous effort. Things were in general very bad; it did not seem that they could get much worse. However, farseeing men knew they could get very much worse and repeatedly warned the English government. During the forty-five years following union with England, 114 commissions and 61 special committees were instructed to report on the state of Ireland, and without exception their findings prophesied disaster; the main factors were Ireland's rapidly increasing population and inadequate food resources. Even before the famine, part of the population during certain times of the year faced the prospect of starvation.

The warnings of the various special committees—as often happens with the findings of such committees—were totally disregarded. Then, quite suddenly, in 1844, they flashed ominously again through the minds of many men who had chosen to ignore them. In this year, news of a potato blight in North America was reported. The following year, Irish farmers began to notice unfamiliar signs of rot in their own potato plants.

"A Fearful Malady"

The blight had first been noticed in England and on the continent. On August 23, 1845, Dr. John Lindley, a professor of botany, wrote, "A fearful malady has broken out among the potato crop. On all sides we hear of the destruction. In Belgium the fields are said to be completely desolated. There is hardly a sound sample in Covent Garden market. . . . As for cure for this distemper, there is none. . . . We are visited by a great calamity which we must bear."

Although the English government publicly suggested that the blight would be contained to certain areas, it was deeply concerned about Ireland's food supply if the disease attacked the Irish crop; no other people in Europe were as dependent on the potato as were the Irish.

When Irish potatoes began to rot—as they soon did—the English considered various measures to stave off famine in Ireland. This, in turn, led to a reconsideration of the corn laws, which had long been a political issue in England. These were laws concerning duties on the importing of foreign grain, which protected the price of grain grown in England; they were staunchly upheld by all English farmers, landowners, and their representatives in Parliament. Consequently, repeal of the corn laws was a serious political issue with which the Tory government, then in power, did not wish to tamper. It attempted to deal with the approaching famine by sending a team of scientists to Ireland who sought some means of salvaging some nourishment from the potato crop. After putting forth several complicated and idiotic suggestions about ways to deal with the problem, they returned to England, and the Irish were left to face the approaching winter without adequate food.

Toward the end of October, new warnings were sent to the English government by men who were foresighted enough to see what horrors were ahead. Lord Monteagle wrote Sir Robert Peel, Prime Minister of England, that he did not "recollect any former example of a calamitous failure being anything near so great and alarming as the present . . . I

Digging peat near Antrim. Fuel is always available even for the poorest people

know not how the peasantry will get through the winter in very many cases."

Finally Sir Robert decided that he must ask for repeal of the corn laws if he was to save Ireland from famine. Hostility from within his own party forced him to resign, but when the opposing party (Whigs) could not form a government, Queen Victoria insisted that he remain in power. Peel spent a hundred thousand pounds on Indian corn (maize) from the United States, which was to alleviate the first year of hunger; unfortunately, this foreign food was most unpalatable to the Irish.

Peel had been forced to choose this grain because it did not interfere with private enterprise; Indian corn had never been imported before and was not known as a food in Ireland or England. The people hadn't the slightest idea of how it could be made fit for human consumption.

Even six months after the potato blight had first appeared, when several areas of the country were already starving, some could not force themselves to eat this distasteful new food. Crude, and difficult to digest, it must have seemed particularly odious to people who were ill, for soon after the famine began, dysentery and fever began to affect many people.

Before long, the number of evictions began to mount; large numbers of people no longer had any income or any hope of an income. Landlords, who saw that land which had been given to the cultivation of potatoes might now be profitably put to grazing cattle, used every excuse to get the tenants off the land and destroy their cottages. When this happened, the peasants took refuge in what was called a "scalp." This was a hole, about two or three feet deep, that was dug into the earth and roofed over with sticks and pieces of turf.

As conditions worsened, the starving people purchased every ounce of the Indian grain that could be had; but the small amount that the government had purchased could not possibly feed a population which at this time numbered over eight million people.

Incredibly, throughout the years of famine, large quantities of food were exported from Ireland. John Mitchel, the Irish revolutionary, wrote that during this period a ship sailing into an Irish port ". . . was sure to meet six ships sailing out with a similar cargo." Such an injustice naturally outraged the Irish, who, when possible, and with the pitiful means at their disposal, attempted to stop the flow of food out of the country. Once again, British arms protected the rights of property owners; in a report to higher officials, a commissariat officer wrote on April 24, 1846, "The barges leave Clonmel once a week for this place, with the export supplies under convoy which, last Tuesday, consisted of 2 gun, 50 cavalry and 80 infantry escorting them on the banks of the Suir as far as Carrick."

By 1846, when the potato blight, much to everyone's horror, had reappeared, Sir Robert Peel was no longer at the head of the government, and those responsible for Ireland's well-being decided against interfering with private enterprises. No food was to be imported or distributed by the government.

Famine

When the starving people began to riot, British troops fired. Still more troops were sent to Ireland and more armed protection given to food being exported from the country. As the winter of 1846 approached, the situation became desperate. The following passage from the autobiography of Father Peter O'Leary describes the heartbreaking end for a family he had befriended—Paddy Buckly, his wife, Kate, and their two children, Sheela and Dairmuid.

Then came the famine, and Sheela, her father, mother and little Dairmuid had to go down to Macroom and enter the Workhouse. As soon as they were inside they were separated. The father was put among the men, the mother among the women. Sheela was put with the little girls and little Dairmuid with the infants. The whole workhouse and all the poor people in it were swamped with every sort of serious illness . . . dying as soon as the disease struck them. There was no room for half of them. Those who could not get in merely lay out on the river bank below the bridge. You saw them there every morning after the night out, stretched in rows, some moving and some very still with no stir from them. Later people came and carried them up to a place near Carrigastary where a big, wide, deep pit was open for them, and thrust them all together into the pit. The same was done with those who were dead in the Workhouse after the night.

The father and mother questioned as much as they could about Sheela and Little Dairmuid. . . . When they found that the two children were already dead, they became so miserable and lonely that they would not stay in the place. They were separated, but they managed to communicate with one another. They agreed on escaping. Patrick slipped out of the house first. He stood waiting at the top of Bothnar na Sop for Kate. After a time he saw her coming, but she walked very slowly. She had the disease. They continued up toward Carrigastary and came to the place where the big pit was. They knew their two children were below in the pit with the hundreds of other bodies. They stayed by the pit and wept for a long time. Above in Derrylea, west of Cahireen, was the little hut where they had lived before they went into the poor house. They left the big pit and went northwest towards Derrylea where the hut was. It was six miles away and night was coming but they kept on. They were hungry and Kate was ill. They had to walk very slowly. When they had gone a couple of miles Kate had to stop. She could go no further. They met neighbours. They were given a drink and a little food, but no one would let them in because they had come direct from the poorhouse, and the wife was ill. Paddy took his wife up on his back and continued toward the hut. . . .

Next day a neighbor came to the hut. He saw the two of them dead and his wife's feet clasped in Paddy's bosom as though he were trying to warm them. It would seem that he felt the death agony come on Kate and had felt her legs grow cold, so he put them inside his own shirt to take the chill from them.

By now this scene—or similar ones—were occurring daily throughout Ireland. Dysentery and typhus were raging throughout the country. Large numbers of people were too weak to work even when jobs were available —and the British had now hurriedly organized various public works that attempted (ineffectually) to give some of the people a chance to earn their livelihood.

Lych gate, formerly used as a rest stop for coffin-bearers

And yet, although the agony of famine was to continue until the end of the decade, when possible, the Irish tried to live as they had before 1845. Mrs. Asenath Nicholson, an American Protestant missionary who had gone to Ireland to run a soup kitchen for the starving, has left a moving account of a Sunday dance at which she was a guest. She writes:

> The cabin was too small to contain the three score and ten who had assembled, and with one simultaneous movement, without speaking, all rushed out, bearing me along, and placed me upon a cart before the door, the player at my right hand. And then a dance began which, to say nothing of the day, was to me of no ordinary kind. Not a laugh—not a loud word was heard; no affected airs, which the young are prone to assume; but as soberly as though they were in a funeral procession, they danced for an hour, wholly for my amusement, and for my welcome. Then each approached, gave me the hand, bade me God speed, leaped over the style, and in stillness walked away. It was a true and hearty Irish welcome in which the aged as well as the young participated.

However, most people who now visited Ireland were saddened by an immense silence that seemed to have settled over the land. Impulsive singing and dancing became very infrequent. A great fear had taken hold of the Irish, which became so intense during these terrible years that for many only one means of survival seemed open to them—flight from Ireland.

Emigration

Before the famine, the idea of leaving Ireland was considered the most terrible thing that could happen to an Irishman. But now it seemed that the island and its people were doomed. Many people at this time did not speak English. Communications were primitive; large numbers of people who did not understand what was happening thought that Ireland was under the curse of God. This was when the great migration began to America, and also to England. It was to continue long after the famine had stopped.

Donald S. Connery writes:

> For generations, Ireland's greatest export has been people. Not just any people, but usually the best people; the youngest, the brightest, the most able and ambitious. They are still leaving the Irish Republic at the rate of a thousand every two or three weeks. A decade ago it was a thousand a week.

Until very recently, the likelihood of emigration hung over the heads of the vast majority of young Irish men and women. Today most of them view the prospect of leaving the country with ambivalence. When they do leave, it is a sad parting, for family ties are strong. In the southwest of the country, going-away parties for young people are still sometimes referred to as "wakes." And yet, this sadness is tempered by a natural curiosity about the world beyond Ireland, a curiosity that recently has been whetted by television, which has brought information about that world into the most remote Irish cottage.

A village forge. Small industries still flourish and trades are handed down from father to son

Many of the young people who leave the country have begun to look forward to an escape from the rigid conventions of Irish society; the world beyond Ireland may appear to be sinful and corrupt, but it cannot help but arouse the interest of young people, who feel more and more that the rather inflexible patterns of Irish society must be adapted to modern life.

The constant emigration of young people has for many years caused Ireland to have a falling birth rate. (It has begun to edge up slightly in the last few years.) But emigration is only one reason for this. The other major factor is, of course, the Irish reluctance to marry, or the custom of marrying late. But whatever the causes, the decline is a matter of great importance to the government.

At the same time, emigration is something of a safety valve for the government because it siphons off large numbers of people who, if they were forced to remain in Ireland, would be unemployed, dissatisfied, and potentially a dangerous threat to the status quo.

Most of the emigrants now go to England; they are for the most part unskilled young people who take jobs as domestics, in construction, road building, or similar trades. The laboring Irish are sometimes referred to by the English as "blacks with a brogue"—an attitude that clearly underscores the prejudice that still exists in England toward the Irish.

Before World War II, most emigrants went to the United States. They would still come if it were not for the new restrictions, which make it almost impossible for anyone to become a resident of this country unless he has a guarantee of a job.

Although the pay in England is lower than in the United States, there are important benefits from working so close to Ireland. The Dublin-London flight takes just eighty-five minutes. This makes it much easier, and far cheaper, to visit home. There are also no passport or visa complications because the Birtish have given special privileges to the Irish, even though Ireland is not a member of the British Commonwealth. Work permits are not required.

Recently, emigration has begun to cause some problems in the labor force at home. Farmers are beginning to complain that they are

Sheepshearer in County Down. Low wages are paid for agricultural work

unable to get help. The problem here is not only the low wages but the repugnance that many Irish feel toward the rural life. Girls are no longer willing to be domestics in Ireland when they can do the same work in England for considerably more money and with the prospect of unlimited personal freedom.

The Returning Emigrant

The emigrant who has spent several years abroad and then returns to Ireland permanently, or even for a short stay, is not a very popular figure. He will be welcomed cordially, of course; he will be given a warm homecoming, with much ringing laughter and good fellowship, but as time goes on, an undercurrent of resentment, unspoken but very real, is likely to spring up toward him.

Very likely, he has prospered abroad. Probably he has a clear memory of the hard life he had while living in Ireland and which is still

Aran Island mother and son. Family ties are strong in remote areas

the lot of many friends and relatives. Often he will subtly, but nevertheless clearly, make known his new, more affluent, state. Sometimes he will also express disapproval of the conditions in Ireland, a land that does not encourage people to make material progress as quickly as they might in other countries.

Such an attitude naturally creates resentment among family, friends, and acquaintances at the local pub. To most of these people, money is still considered a vulgar commodity that one is forced to deal with—but would rather not. Soon they see other changes in their visitor: he is not as amusing as he once was; his voice has become loud and brash and religion is no longer as important to him as it had been before he went abroad.

When he learns how his friends feel about him, the returning emigrant is naturally disturbed. He finds himself with an ambivalent attitude toward his homeland. He knows that his help is badly needed, and in most cases he will continue to be as conscientious about his financial responsibilities as he was in the past. (Without frequent remittances from abroad, a large number of Irish families would be forced into serious economic difficulties.) He feels drawn to the places of his childhood and to his strict religious obligations. But now a new way of life has opened up before him, a new freedom and new values have been revealed. To give up this unfamiliar but intriguing life is difficult, and the majority of emigrant Irishmen choose not to do it.

When living abroad, the Irish—even though they may have lived in the country for several generations—remain labeled as Irish. President Kennedy's father once said, "I was born in the United States and so was my father before me but my children are still called Irish. What the hell do we have to do to become Americans?"

Actually, the continuing sense of national identity is a common characteristic of minority peoples. The Parsis of India, the Jewish people in many parts of the world, and many other minorities have instinctively sensed that if they are to nourish and perpetuate their traditions, they must work to maintain that sense of identity. What sets the Irish apart is the fact that, while usually the clannishness grows from within the minority, with the Irish, it seems imposed from without.

Family Life and Pastimes

Irish family life is known for the warm attachments the different members of a family are likely to have for each other; in particular, brothers and sisters often feel a sense of responsibility toward one another that is rare among most other peoples. These warm bonds of kinship contribute much toward a sense of security within a family. Many observers of the Irish scene have found that beneath these admirable attitudes is a deep-seated fear of leaving the security of the family situation for the more responsible and more demanding role of a husband or wife.

The thirty-five-year-old farmer's son who says that he must help his aged parents, or his only surviving sister, has often refused to face the fact that he simply does not want to get married. He does not want the paternal, economic, and sexual responsibilities marriage involves. To this day, a quarter of all Irishmen do not marry at all.

William Irwin Thompson has written:

> In that [Irish] culture, virginity is considered a higher state than marriage, and the brother who becomes a priest is a greater and stronger man than the brother who, out of carnal weakness, marries; the sister who becomes a nun is closer to God because of the offering up of her barren womb; and over all the sexual occasions of human life, a celibate clergy keeps insistent watch.

A vast proportion of Irishmen do not marry until their thirtieth

Boys enjoy the bustle of market day in Ennis, County Clare

Even in sophisticated Dublin, families are large, and the older children help care for younger ones

birthday, and many marry considerably later than that. For a woman the average age is twenty-seven. It is said that many thousands of Irish girls who leave the country every year do so not only to find a higher standard of living but as well to find husbands.

Some Irishmen explain the situation by saying that the problem is mainly a matter of economics. Before the famine, the Irish married early and produced a large number of children. Since that time, this viewpoint maintains, the economic burdens of matrimony have loomed so ominously on the horizon of any young man that he simply found it easier to put the whole thing out of his head.

The fact is that prior to the famine the birth rate throughout *all* of Europe was soaring (historians are still not exactly sure of the reasons). And the second refutation of this reasoning is that it does not explain why the Irish who are well off also prefer to marry late.

The unmarried daughter who chooses to remain on the farm to look after her brothers or father is a familiar figure in Ireland. And often brothers and sisters will remain together after their parents have died. An article in the journal of the Irish Medical Association spoke of the "pathological constellation, not uncommon in Ireland . . . where both parents are dead and gone, but several brothers and sisters are still clinging together into middle age. If one asks, 'Why did you never marry?' the response often is, 'Oh, I couldn't, I had to look after my brothers.' "

The attachment between an Irish mother and her son is particularly strong. But even in a relationship as close as this, both individuals refrain from outwardly showing affection. Emotions are generally hidden because it is felt that such displays are not proper. One woman said, "There's no kissing in public in this country and none at home either if there are children present."

Fathers are not very deeply involved with their children when they are very young; but by the time a boy is seven or eight, the average father's attitude changes and he begins to spend much more time with his son.

In a good many Irish country homes, the wife eats her dinner only after the men have eaten theirs and left the table. Her life is generally closely restricted to domestic affairs; even pleasures outside the home are participated in separately by the husband and wife. It is the men and sons who go off to the village pub together, who attend hurling and football matches together. In some small-town churches, men and boys sit separately from the women and girls.

The very mention of the word "sex" seems to shock and embarrass a large number of Irish people. The sexual function is regarded as a fearful thing synonymous with sin. This obsession is carried to such extremes that Irish newspapers, when referring to the artificial insemination of farm animals, use only the initials, "A. I."

Sex education is nonexistent; divorce is prohibited, as are all forms of birth control.

In 1934, H. V. Morton wrote,

> I realize in Connaught one feature of the English landscape which
> is seldom or never seen in Ireland; a courting couple. In England

boys and girls, arm in arm, are met with on every country road, or you see groups of country lads and lassies walking out together. In Ireland, as I noted in Kerry, the separateness of the sexes is remarkable. Love is perhaps in Ireland not a sentimental obsession as it is in England. In Connaught and the west generally, men seldom marry for love; they marry, to some extent, for land.

Segregation of the sexes is still the rule in Irish life. Most primary schools are under the control of the parish priests, and even at this early age every effort is made to keep the sexes apart. As boys and girls grow older, the segregation is more strictly enforced, until by the time they are teenagers a definite abyss—and one that becomes increasingly difficult to cross—has been created. At most dances, girls sit near the walls, while the boys congregate near the door or in other groups from which they make tentative moves toward a girl from time to time.

An Aran Island woman invites tourists into her cottage, where she is spinning wool for sweaters

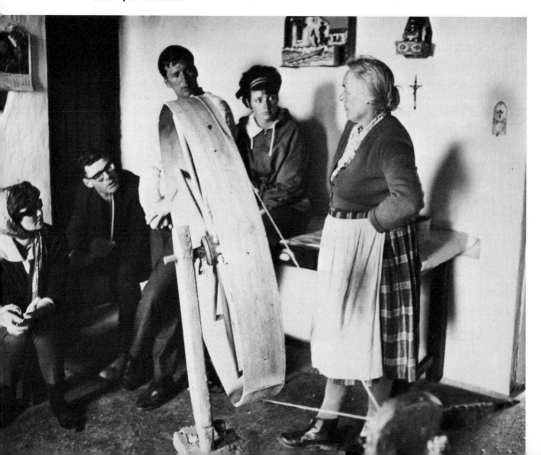

Young people, even after they have left school, tend to remain with their families whenever possible. This limits the privacy that young people can have together, and as cars are still much too expensive for most of them, the mobility and privacy of having their own automobile is an experience few have.

Financial limitations contribute to the continued segregation of sexes in other ways. Because there is just not very much money to spend on at the pub with the men. It's the only place a young man can have companionship for little money.

Within the house (a country cottage or cabin, as they are often called), the atmosphere is usually one of simplicity and frugality. About 35,000 of the 200,000 farms have a television set. Although few families have refrigerators, the damp and frequently cold climate make their use not the necessity they are in warmer countries.

There are few homes that do not have religious pictures on the walls. Very often a red light burns before the Sacred Heart. Often the picture may be a grocer's calendar showing Christ in benediction, carrying a lamb.

The heat invariably comes from a turf fire. After visiting a country cottage, H. V. Morton wrote:

> The soul of these cabins is the generous turf fire burning in an open hearth. I know of no heat more social, more gentle, more appealing in some way to the affection and imagination. Burning turf is almost like living presence in the room. It pervades a house. The scent of it lies around a house and promises warmth and shelter to any traveller outside in the open; the pungence of it lives on in your clothes and reminds you days afterward of the kindness and hospitality of an Irish home.

Hospitality is an old tradition in Ireland. Unlike many countries of Europe, where many years can pass before one is asked into a home, the Irish may astonish you by inviting you to tea or a meal soon after meeting. The easy flow of conversation, the lack of hurry, and the genuine interest in the visitor often create an atmosphere of great warmth and charm. And this is as true of urban areas as it is in the countryside. Kevin O'Casey of Dublin is used to having people around him—not only his many brothers and sisters but friends as well.

Kevin O'Casey of Dublin

This teen-age boy lives in a middle-class section of Dublin not far from Ballsbridge, where the great annual horse show is held. His father works in the office of the Guinness Brewery, and his mother—like most Irish women—stays close to home and concerns herself mainly with domestic matters. He has two sisters and three brothers; Kevin is the eldest. Like many other Irish children who are older than their brothers or sisters, he feels a sense of responsibility toward them, particularly the boys.

The Catholic religion is the foundation of Kevin's life; his earliest memories are of lying in his bed and seeing the brightly colored picture of Christ on the opposite wall. A Sunday has never passed without his attending church, and often he has asked himself if he would like to become a monk or a priest. Religion is also a part of his school life, which is under the supervision of the Jesuits. Last year, when Kevin's uncle had some serious problems that Kevin never understood. very well, the parish priest was frequently in the house talking to his father. Soon afterward, Kevin's uncle went away for several months to a monastery, where the monks helped him with his problem. When serious difficulties arise in Kevin's family, even those not connected with religion, the man his people turn to for advice is their priest.

Kevin's constant awareness of the authority of the Church and its personification in the priest has gradually nurtured a submissive attitude that is characteristic of the Irish people. Kevin speaks softly and with deference to the priest, his teachers, and his parents. Kevin is respectful when dealing with anyone in a position of authority.

Of course, like all other boys his age, Kevin has his share of fights, minor squabbles, and outbursts of anger, but they are confined to his contemporaries. Much of his emotion is expressed on the playing field.

Kevin has lived in the city all his life, but neither he nor his family feel bothered by the restriction of their urban environment. Dublin, unlike so many other European cities, is spacious. There are many trees,

92

In residential Dublin, there is always a Catholic church nearby and at least one boy practicing football in the street

and the air is fresh and clean. Kevin and his father and brothers spend much time on the nearby playing fields, and just a twenty-minute drive to the south stretch some of Dublins best beaches. Although Kevin's father was born on a farm in County Clare and came to Dublin as a young man, he feels no nostalgia for country life and does not speak of it with fond memories. The family have all moved from the area, and Kevin and his brothers have never seen County Clare.

Kevin's great passion is Gaelic football; when not playing it himself, he follows the progress of the various professional leagues. Because of his interest in sports, Kevin is strong and lean. Sometimes the idea of becoming a priest or monk seems much too remote or unreal; becoming a professional football player seems much more within his grasp. But often that, too, seems fanciful. There is time to think about all that. The important thing, as his parents and the priests tell him, is to study hard and observe the dictates of his religion.

93

Donkeys in Connemara are beasts of burden as well as subjects for tourists' cameras

Kathleen Kelly of Connemara

Kathleen lives in Connemara about thirty miles north of the city of Galway, in the west of Ireland. She has known poverty intimately all her life, as have her parents and their parents before them. It is the kind of poverty with which much of Ireland has been familiar for centuries. But, while a great many other sections of Ireland have begun to prosper or, at least, to lift themselves from the terrible abyss of abject poverty, Connemara, beautiful, barren, and remote, is still terribly, desperately poor.

Kathleen is thirteen. Although her clothes show immediate evidence of how little money her family has, her body is strong and healthy, her eyes are clear, her complexion is radiant. For these she must thank the very plainness of her life—the fresh, clean, moist air, which is not polluted, the clear, unadulterated water from a nearby stream, the heathy cow that produces a large amount of milk every day. Kathleen's diet is limited but adequate. It consists mainly of potatoes, but dairy products contribute other important nutrients. A frequent bit of meat (or occasionally, fish), an orange or an apple round out this monotonous but sufficient diet of the poor.

Kathleen's family lives in only two rooms. As is typical of the smaller farmhouses of County Galway, one room serves as a kitchen-living room, the other is a tiny bedroom. The open fire is at floor level, and the chimney is solidly built of stone. The Kellys make do with the barest essentials of furniture, dishes, and other household items. There has never been any question of buying beautiful things, or indulging in any luxuries. Entertainment is limited to an occasional visit to Galway and perhaps a tour of the shops (but not to buy), a motion picture, a cup of tea, or an ice cream.

What little outside money has been coming into Connemara is due partly to the rustic charm of its cottages and the harsh but beautiful land. More and more such unspoiled places as Connemara have begun to appeal to city-weary tourists who are prepared to put up with very simple accommodations in order to enjoy the unsullied beauty and peace of the land. They come only in the summer, and since the summer is a short period here, most months of the year go by without the income of any tourist dollars. (Although the Kellys do not receive such money directly, they inevitably profit from the boost in the local economy when summer comes.)

Kathleen's father was injured two years ago, but the government pays him an allowance—as it does thousands of other people in the west of Ireland—to maintain the Irish language. This, together with the money Kathleen's mother earns working in a hotel kitchen during the summer months, brings in all the income the family has. And yet, even though their income is extremely low, there are many compensations that make their simple way of life far more attractive than the existence of urban people with similar incomes.

Kathleen and her small brother are able to collect enough turf for the family's needs. She has been going to collect it from the small bog five miles from her home for almost as long as she can remember. This turf provides heat for the family throughout the year. Kathleen, although she has seen an occasional snowfall, has never known the snow to remain on the ground overnight. Far more serious are the North Atlantic gales that in the winter sometimes howl for days along the Connemara coast. But even through the worst of these, the turf fire keeps the family warm.

The house is snug and cozy, and food is plentiful. Like the vast majority of the Irish who have a small plot of land, Kathleen's family grow their own potatoes, which form the basis of the daily diet. Usually they are eaten with large amounts of butter; occasionally onions vary the dish. Milk and buttermilk are provided by their cow.

Although Kathleen is very fond of her home, she has heard a great deal about life in England and America from friends and relatives who have emigrated. From what they write, and talk about, when they come home to visit, life in these other countries seems very different—much faster, more complex, and often difficult.

These stories have aroused Kathleen's curiosity and interest. How nice it would be to have money to buy things—all the pretty things that Kathleen has never been able to have. In three years Katheen will be sixteen, and then she will be able to join that long exodus of young people who have for centuries been leaving Ireland. She is certain to get a job abroad that would pay her more than she could earn in Ireland. She will try living in England or America for a year or two, and perhaps by that time, when she returns to Ireland, jobs will be more plentiful and salaries higher. Already salaries are rising.

Sean Delaney of Belfast

Sean Delaney lives in a prosperous suburb of Belfast. His is the tradition of the Orangemen, the Protestants (descended from the English) who form the larger part of the population of Belfast. Sean's mother does not work; she finds her husband's substantial salary adequate for the family's needs. Sean, who is thirteen, has an older sister of twenty, who works as a secretary in one of the companies that manufacture supplies for the Belfast shipbuilding industry; it is a good job, and her salary is also adequate. Unlike thousands of Irish girls who

Steaming up Belfast Lough toward the docks. The capital of Northern Ireland is also a busy port and shipbuilding center

live in the Republic, she has never had any plans to emigrate from Ireland.

Sean's father works in the linen industry, which for centuries has made Belfast famous throughout the world. He works as hard as did his English and Scottish forebears, and he is suspicious of his southern neighbors, who seem to take life much too easily. But this suspicion is not uncommon; his family, neighbors—indeed, the rest of his countrymen—share it. Sean Delaney has grown up in the curious position of deep distrust of most Irishmen. They are Catholic and therefore they are suspect.

Although Sean is well aware of the disorders that have torn Northern Ireland during recent years, he has never had any problems with the Catholics he knows. However, it is not easy to be friends with a Catholic; in Northern Ireland the strong forces of prejudice militate to keep even young children of the two religions apart. The conversations that he has heard between his parents, and when friends or neighbors come to visit, do not help matters. He is confused by the hostility he has begun to feel and does not fully understand.

Since indolence is not tolerated by his teachers or parents, Sean works hard at school and gets good grades. Somehow the fact that a good academic showing is expected of him makes it easier to achieve high scholastic levels. Sean will not attend the university, but he plans to go to one of the excellent trade schools in Belfast and learn a skill that will eventually bring him a good income.

Sometimes the thought of going to America to make his fortune occurs to Sean; he knows—as do all other inhabitants of Belfast—that some of the greatest fortunes in America (including that of the Mellon family) were founded by immigrants from Northern Ireland. Usually, however, such dreams are only a passing fancy, because today there is no real need to emigrate. Sean enjoys the prosperity of Northern Ireland and feels certain that he can contribute to increasing it in the years to come. Such an ambitious attitude is an old tradition here; it is quite probable that Sean will succeed in doing exactly what he plans to do.

Although many serious problems lie ahead for the young people of Northern Ireland, one which threatens a growing number of people throughout the world will probably not affect them in the near future. And that is simply the problem of getting enough to eat.

Food

The Irish, according to United Nations statistics, are better fed than any other people in the world. Still, the reputation of Irish food is not a good one, and the Irish themselves are well aware of foreigners' preconceptions of what they will be eating when they visit Ireland. This reputation is not deserved, for the dishes, although simple and of limited variety, are well prepared, having, blessedly, come not from the freezer, but usually directly from the vegetable garden.

98

Most of the Irish live on pork, bacon, lamb, sausages, cabbage, large amounts of potatoes, some green vegetables, and a small amount of fruit. Meat is plentiful, however, and the lamb is particularly good. Irish bread—both the soda bread and the coarse-grain brown bread—are delicious, but probably bread, sweets, and tea form too large a part of the average diet.

The visitor to Ireland should not expect food seasoned with exotic spices, he must not look for inventive sauces or unique combinations; but if he is willing to accept very simple, fresh food, he will not be disappointed.

The Irish, unlike the continental Europeans, prefer a large breakfast. Often they will have cereal (hot or cold), bacon, eggs or sausages, perhaps a bit of black pudding (steamed spiced pork blood), home-baked bread, and tea.

Lunch is the main meal of the day; it is eaten fairly late—about one or two o'clock. It can be a full four-course dinner with soup, meat, potatoes, one or two vegetables, a dessert, and tea or coffee. Afternoon tea is taken around 4 o'clock. This varies a good deal, depending upon the amount of time you have and your occupation. It can be just a quick cup of tea. If you have enough time, sandwiches or cakes are also eaten. If cheese sandwiches are on the menu, the chances are they will be served with an excellent sharp-flavored cheddar.

High tea is really the evening meal, and it is eaten from 6 to 7 o'clock. There is more fresh-baked bread, butter, and jam, "lashings" of tea, and perhaps cold meats, chops, fish, or salads. Late supper is a light meal, often a snack before bedtime. Once again, tea, bread, butter, and cakes will frequently be eaten, usually with whatever left-over foods from the day remain.

Since Ireland's lush pastures produce possibly the finest beef cattle to be found anywhere, the quality of Irish beef is particularly good. Lamb is excellent, and pork is also of high quality. The most highly prized seafood dish is salmon—poached, grilled, or smoked.

Many varieties of Irish bread are good; some are made of a com-bination of white- and whole-wheat flours, others are dark or have the coarseness of the cracked wheat. Potato bread is famous, of course, as is soda bread. Whatever the variety, Irish bread always has a wholesomeness that tastes delicious.

The fact that these young Irish people are well nourished is obvious to anyone who happens to meet them on their way to or from school. Good color, as mentioned before, is one of their marked characteristics. Glossy hair and bright eyes are still others. Certainly the inevitable walk—and sometimes it is a long one—to and from school contributes to their physical well-being.

Primary, Secondary, and Vocational Schools

The Irish Constitution recognizes that parents are free to provide for the education of their children "in their homes or in private schools or in schools recognized or established by the State." The Department of

Students hurry to lectures at Trinity College. The famous Book of Kells *is on display in the college library*

Education provides for free primary education and contributes funds to secondary or vocational schools and to the universities.

All children in the primary grades attend schools administered by their religion—Catholic, Protestant, or Jewish. Most Irish children attend a state-supported primary school of their own religious denomination.

Secondary schools are private institutions, but they receive government grants. In addition, the state pays over 75 percent of the salaries of registered teachers.

The vocational school system is entirely financed by the state; its services also provide adult education. The proportion of Irish students attending secondary and vocational schools is about the same as that in other Western European countries.

Universities

There are two universities in the Republic. The National University of Ireland is a Catholic institution; the other university, both older and more famous, is the University of Dublin, better known as Trinity College.

Trinity College, which was founded in 1591, is in the heart of Dublin and is the only remaining monument of the Elizabethan age in the city. Stephen Swynn writes in *The Famous Cities of Ireland:*

> Its foundation is the first real landmark in the Dublin that we know—the metropolis of Ireland; and it expresses the positive or constructive side of Elizabethan rule. English statesmen had now fully determined to make Ireland into a Protestant nation. From the beginning of the seventeenth century onwards the university has been there, not cloistered and apart like those of Oxford and Cambridge, on whose model it was planned, but making a part of the metropolitan life.

Of the buildings and stonework comprising the first Trinity College almost nothing remains, but succeeding buildings were copies of the original. The library, handsomely designed by Thomas Burgh, has one of the largest reading rooms in the world. Many famous men of letters have studied and written in this beautiful building, among them Oliver Goldsmith and Jonathan Swift. There are many traditions and superstitions connected with the college. Some students still avoid sitting under the portrait of Queen Elizabeth I in the Examination Hall, which is known for its unlucky atmosphere.

There was no exclusion of students on religious grounds before Charles I, and for many generations now religion has had no part in determining acceptance of a student by the College. In the past, the Catholic Church did not permit Catholics to attend Trinity without the permission of their bishop; however, this hundred-year-old ban was lifted in June of 1970.

Trinity has been completely nondenominational since 1873 (earlier than Cambridge and Oxford opened their doors to students of all religions). Today a quarter of all students are Catholic. A favorite joke of Dublin taxicab drivers—spoken to amuse English visitors primarily, is, "And there's Trinity College where you can study any bloody religion you like."

Although Trinity offers courses in Irish for those interested, the language is of far less importance there than in other Irish place of learning.

Irish Language

The importance of the Irish (or Gaelic) language in the developing Irish nation is the subject of a continuing controversy among Irishmen. Today, in order to enter the Civil Service, it is necessary to have some measure of fluency in Irish, and those who take their other subjects in Irish get a 10 percent bonus on their grades. In two government departments, the Department of the Gaeltacht and Education, Irish is used for all everyday business. If civil servants wish to apply for promotion, they must take further tests in Irish.

It is necessary to have some knowledge of the language for those entering the police force and especially for those who are interested in promotion. In the army, commands are still given in Irish.

Approximately half of Ireland's secondary schools (that is, schools attended by students between twelve and nineteen years of age) teach at least some other subjects in Irish. Some of them use Irish as the sole means of instruction, although these are gradually diminishing in number. In most of the other schools, Irish is taught in much the same way that French, Spanish, or any other foreign language is taught; students learn to read and write it moderately well and are able to pass examinations. They are not, and do not hope to become, conversationally fluent. Only at the University of Galway is it possible to do *all* of one's work in Irish.

Many people are bitterly opposed to the time and money spent in efforts to keep the Irish language alive. They argue that its costs far outweigh its advantages, that although it was important to nourish the dying language until Ireland finally achieved independence, the

Direction signs in County Cork are in Gaelic and English

country would be wiser to direct its energies toward a greater internationalism.

Staunch nationalists refute this claim; they remember very well the difficulties that were encountered when they tried to find enough teachers who were proficient in the language to teach it to others after Ireland had gained her independence. Those who had some knowledge of Irish tried to spend as much time as possible in the few remaining districts where it was still spoken. In addition to the main object of revivifying the dying language was added a monetary incentive for any teacher able to teach in Irish: Such teachers were given a 10 percent increase in their salaries.

Another serious problem during this time was the scarcity of books in Irish. Those that existed were old and not suited to modern teaching methods. It would take time for new texts to be prepared, printed, and distributed.

During those first days of the new Republic, the nationalists hoped that Irish would become the first official language of the country. Although they realized that English was extremely important, they felt that it might be used for commerce or generally as a second language in much the same way the Swedes or Danes use it today. Road signs were changed to show the Irish first, the English underneath. Public lavatories must have been a problem for foreign visitors, for they had only the signs *Mna* (Men) or *Fir* (Women). All this has now been changed, of course.

In 1951, in spite of all efforts, the Dublin Institute of Advanced Studies concluded that "no more than 35,000 people now use Irish as their ordinary medium of speech and no more than 300 are ignorant of English."

Today, although most people who once favored the return to Irish have now reversed their opinions, the government still spends a considerable amount of money in keeping the language alive—perhaps as much as 2 or 3 percent of the national budget.

The construction of an Irish sentence is entirely different from an English one. If you are accustomed to think in Irish, it is practically impossible to keep some of the Irish rhythm from getting into the

English translation of what you are saying. Many people who laugh when they hear an Irishman's curious phrases are unaware that he is merely giving them a direct translation of perfectly correct Irish idioms.

Another difficulty is presented by the vowel sounds. In Irish they are special and distinct. Each one is given its full value and each one is sounded separately in much the same way as in Greek. For example, two Greek words which appear in the Latin of the Mass, kyrie eleison, are pronounced kir-ee-ay ay-lay-ee-son. Irish vowels must be said just as carefully. Another example of this is the English words "faith" and "boat." English and Americans would say fayth and bote, but the Irish say fay-ith and bo-at.

Although you will hear the Irish voice all about you in the usual walks of life, there is no better place to be exposed to its full range of lyricism and polemic (except for the theater) than in the pub.

The Pub

The pub is a well-known and important feature of Irish life; it is so world famous that no visitor to Ireland feels he has really seen the country until he has visited at least one or two pubs—and there are pubs for every taste.

At one time, most pubs were dark and uncomfortable. Many had bare wooden floors often covered with sawdust. Many were dirty and ill kept, but that is now completely changed. Most are comfortable, warm, some have fireplaces, and an increasing number boast television sets—a dire threat to the tradition of good pub conversation. Some pubs are noisy and smoky, filled with songs and colorful conversation. Others are dignified, quiet places, which do not tolerate such behavior. Some are restricted to male clientele; a growing number have sections that permit both men and women. The Irish believe that drinking at home is boring and antisocial; this includes even the upper classes, who, in most countries, prefer to do their drinking in private.

There are many theories about the Irish predilection for liquor. Some writers believe that alcholism developed in the nineteenth century because of the despair of poverty and political oppression that weighed so heavily on the lives of the people. They drank in order to

The local pub is an important part of an Irishman's social life. Dubliners gather to talk and drink at McDaid's Bar

find oblivion. But this theory does not explain why so many Irish who have emigrated (and now have much higher incomes) also have a high percentage of alcoholism.

"The Irishman takes his drink sadly," wrote Arland Ussher in *The Face and Mind of Ireland.* "It is like a mournful symbol that even his beer is black. He drinks to attain forgetfulness of the whole human condition—that condition to which he feels so exceedingly ill-adapted."

George Bernard Shaw thought that the Irishman's extraordinary imagination was the reason for his love of liquor. "An Irishman's imagination never lets him alone," Shaw wrote, "never convinces him, never satisfies him; but it makes him that he can't face reality nor deal with it nor handle it nor conquer it; he can only sneer at them that do . . . imagination's such a torture that you can't bear it without whiskey."

Alcoholism remains a serious problem in Ireland, but the widespread drunkenness of former periods has disappeared. The staggering drunk, trying to find his way through the city's streets, is now an uncommon sight. One of the restrictions that has helped to make him scarce is the high tax on whiskey, which has placed it beyond the reach of most Irishmen as a steady drink. Stout, the national drink, has less alcoholic content, and therefore more of it is required to get really soused. (Stout is a beer but almost black in color.)

Although such figures are shocking for those not familiar with Irish ways, the Irish themselves are not surprised by the fact that a village such at Milltown Malbay in County Clare, with a population of only 650 people, has 27 licensed pubs or public bars.

Until recently, the St. Patrick's Day law demanded that bars be closed on this holy day. The only one that could be opened was the bar at the traditional St. Patrick's Day Dog Show in Dublin. Wits had it that this was the reason for the vast popularity of this show and the great rush it attracted. One year Brendan Behan, the famous Irish playwright, accidentally stepped on the paw of a terrier on its way to the judging circle. Indignantly the dramatist glared at the dog's owner and said, "Now isn't this a silly place to bring a dog?"

It would be a mistake to equate the Irish pub with the bars of other countries. Although the average Irishman may spend more time there than his counterpart in other parts of the world, what draws him night after night is not only the liquor—and perhaps not the liquor at all in some cases—but the warmth and camaraderie of his friends and the special atmosphere of ease and relaxation he associates with the pub. An Irishmen usually has a favorite pub; when he is joined there by his friends, it is as much a club as a pub.

The Irish emphasize this aspect of pub life; they point out that the common drink of the country is not whiskey but the black Guinness stout or lager beer. They claim that the familiar picture of the Irish alcoholic is much exaggerated and may apply to Irish expatriates far more than to the Irish at home—and there is much evidence they may be right.

All Ireland Hurling Finals between Tipperary and Kilkenny

Occasionally you will come across an Irishman wearing a small Sacred Heart badge in his lapel; it means that he is a member of the Pioneer Total Abstinence Association of the Sacred Heart. Members who have taken a vow of abstinence now number over half a million people and as such form a large part of the population.

Although there are few subjects you will not hear discussed at the pub, two are sure to be dominant: politics and sports and of the two, sports is probably the favorite.

Sports

The Irish are passionately interested in sports; indeed, some observers have suggested that the country would profit considerably if some of the competitive energy now devoted to sports could be directed to other areas of life. It is a point worthy of much thought by the Irish, for it appears that an enormous amount of ambition has been directed to the vicarious pleasures of the sporting event.

Poverty, lack of resources, lack of challenge and opportunities to develop culturally and economically have forced the Irish to direct their creativity into certain limited channels. The Irish are known as great lovers of sports, but they are in fact primarily attracted to the spectator sports through which, apparently, their tensions and restrained emotions are released. That the average Irishman—and woman—is in good physical condition is not due to his participation in sports but to his agricultural life and the relatively small number of automobiles in Ireland.

On Sunday afternoons during the summer or autumn months, the Irish will attend hurling or football matches. County hurling and football teams are amateur organizations. After the provincal elimination games, the national championship games are held in September at Croke Park in Dublin, where they attract crowds of eighty thousand or more.

Hurling is a kind of field hockey; it is played with a thick, curved stick of ash, and a small ball. To play it well requires a good sense of timing and much skill. It is a fast, exciting game, which has been played in Ireland for hundreds of years.

From the spectator's point of view, hurling looks like a cross between a shillelagh fight and a highly dangerous, high-speed version of hockey. The hurley—a stout, unsprung ashplant—is swinging high in the air a good deal of the time. Gaelic football is also very fast; it is played with a round ball, like soccer, but the ball is bounced and handled as well as kicked. There are fifteen men on each squad.

Another game that fascinates the Irish is Gaelic football, which is now more popular than hurling. A combination of Rugby and soccer, it permits charging and long kicking but no tackling. Both hurling and Gaelic football were prohibited in past years by the British because of their Irish character and the possibility that they might arouse or stimulate Irish nationalist fervor. In 1884, an association called the Gaelic Athletic Association was organized to revive interest in the game; one of its rules was to forbid any member of its teams to play British sports such as soccer, Rugby, or cricket. The intensity of anti-British feeling at the time can be gained from another rule, now relaxed, which forbade its members to even *watch* non-Irish sports.

Dogs and Dog Racing

The Irish wolfhound was orginally bred as a hunter of deer and wolves. The first references to this dog are found in ancient Celtic history. The first written account was in A.D. 391, when Quintus Aurelius Symmachus, a Roman consul, wrote to his brother Flavianus:

> In order to win the favor of the Roman people for our Quaestor you have been a generous and diligent provider of novel contributions to our solemn shows and game, as is proved by your gift of seven Irish dogs. All Rome viewed them with wonder, and fancied they must have been brought hither in iron cages. For such a fight, I tender you the greatest possible thanks.

They are also mentioned in the Icelandic saga of Burnt Njal, in which Olaf, the Norwegian son of an Irish princess, says to his friend:

> I will give thee a hound that was given to me in Ireland; he is big, and no worse than a stout man. Besides it is part of his nature that he has man's wit and he will bay at every man whom he

110

Pedigree Irish wolfhounds are bred at Glendalough, County Wicklow

knows to be thy foe, but never at thy friends. He can see, too, in any man's face whether he means thee well or ill, and he will lay down his life to be true to thee.

By 1605, the Irish wolfhound was known in many parts of Europe. The dogs became so sought after by the nobility of foreign countries that in 1652 a declaration against their export was proclaimed. By the end of the eighteenth century, the Irish wolfhound had become extremely rare and was, in fact, in danger of becoming extinct.

In the past this dog was a strong and fearless hunter, but the wolfhound of today, although still of great size and commanding appearance, is more a companion dog. Gentle and affectionate, he is an excellent dog for children, but also a good watchdog. He adjusts easily to hot or cold climates.

Most large towns have greyhound-racing tracks. In Dublin, Meath,

Cork, and Tipperary counties—as well as at the National Open Cup Meeting in Kildare—dogs are permitted to race across the open fields.

It is difficult to justify the Irish love of dog and horse racing under sports, although a good many writers choose to do it. Although it may be argued that the development of the breed and the strength and beauty of the greyhounds are factors in this pastime, it appears to the uninvolved observer that the betting is the prime attraction for most enthusiasts.

Ireland is the biggest producer of racing greyhounds in the world. Most of the dogs that race in Britain come from Ireland. Many farmers rear a few greyhounds every year.

Although dog-racing tracks are well attended, the Irishmen's interest in this pastime, or in dogs, is far exceeded by his great enthusiasm for horse breeding and racing.

Horses and Fox Hunting

The horse is the great passion of Ireland. There is not an Irishman, rich or poor, who is not delighted by the sight of a beautiful high-stepping horse as he races through the fields or clatters through a town, his hooves ringing on the cobbles. Should there be a good stud stabled near the town, he will be the local celebrity. Everyone in the town will know his dam and sire and each of his defects and virtues.

"Bloodstock" is a word frequently heard in horse and horse-racing circles. The dictionary defines it as "thoroughbred horses, particularly race horses." For many years the finest horses in the world have come from Ireland.

Of course there are many other reasons for the preeminence of Irish horses, but the most important ones are those two basics: geography and weather. The lush grass of the Irish meadowlands is considered the finest feed in the world; it grows from limestone soil that is common throughout the island. Horses do not require a great deal of sunlight and warmth; on the contrary, they seem to thrive in a moist, cool atmosphere.

The town of Kildare, a busy market town at the western edge of

"Arkle," famous Irish steeplechaser at morning exercise

the Curragh plain, is the center of the Irish horse breeding and training industry. It owes its origin to Saint Brigid, who founded a religious establishment there about A.D. 470.

It was not until the 1890's that Colonel Hall-Walker began to establish what was to become the best stud farm in the world. After considering many parts of the island, he finally settled on a thousand acres of grassland in Tully, County Kildare. It is now the National Stud.

The National Stud (which is the property of the Irish government), breeds, sells, and trains racehorses. Some of the most famous racehorses in the world have come from this source, which is in the heart of the Irish "horse country."

A curious, unexpected treasure found at the National Stud is a Japanese garden, which was designed many years ago by a masterful Japanse landscape designer who required four years and forty-five assistants to construct the garden.

In the great tradition of Japanese gardens, this one tells the story, symbolically, of a man's life from birth to death. It begins in a dark tunnel, which symbolizes birth, followed by straggling steps representing the years between youth and manhood. Next comes a parting of the path, symbolic of the perplexities of early life; then the path winds around rocks, courses streams and a hill, which stands for ambition. Heavily massed flowers, symbolic of a love affair lead to marriage, where two stones are joined together side by side across a stream. The difficulties of married life are symbolized by steps that mount a hill; they are far apart and difficult to climb. Two paths instead of the one, temporarily diverging, indicate a quarrel. Beyond a hill they join again—and so the path goes, beautiful as a garden and haunting as a microcosm of human life.

There are hundreds of stud farms throughout the land—some very large and famous, others almost amateur operations. All encourage the continuing interest in bloodstock.

Young competitors are proud of the ribbon their horse has won at the Dublin Horse Show

Valuable stud stallions are expected to perform their services at least once and often twice a day during the season, which lasts from early February until the middle of June. To keep the studs in top physical condition throughout the year, many of the best stud farms see to it that they have a diet of first-crop hay, corn, flaxseed, and one dozen raw eggs a day.

Hundreds and sometimes thousands of dollars are paid for the services of a stud. Many owners of fine studs will not accept a mare, even at a high stud fee, if they believe that the two bloodlines are not suited to each other; poor progeny do not enhance the stud farm's reputation and no owner wants to do anything that will threaten it.

Horse racing is a very ancient sport in Ireland and is mentioned in several old legends. The first steeplechase was run about two hundred years ago on a cross-country course between the towns of Buttevant and Doneraile in County Cork. The riders jumped or avoided walls, fences, gates, brooks, and other obstacles, all the while keeping the steeple of the church at Doneraile in sight as a landmark to guide them. That's how the new sport received its name.

Throughout most of the history of steeplechasing in England, Irish-bred horses have been the dominant winners. This is also true of the famous Grand National where Irish horses have also dominated the field. Of the fifty-one Grand National races run since the beginning of the century, thirty-five have been won by Irish horses.

Breeding and raising horses requires great skill, and theories are wildly at variance with one another. But it is thought that one of the main reasons Irish horses are of consistently high quality is that they are carefully nurtured and cared for during their early years. On the continent, horses are raced as early as possible. Often at the end of three or four seasons they are retired to the stud farm. Irish horses, although ridden on the hunting fields when they are young, are not forced to endure the same strains and rigors as the continental horses. They enter races when they are older and sometimes reach their highest levels of performance when they are nine or ten years old. Some have won races at the ages of thirteen or fourteen.

The Dublin Horse Show is the greatest sporting and social event of the year; it is held early in August in the Ballsbridge section of Dublin. By far the most festive time of the year, it usually attracts more than a hundred thousand visitors. The show's main event is the International Jumping Competition for the Aga Khan Cup; some of the world's leading teams compete for this prize.

More than one thousand horses—the best Ireland has produced—are entered in the show, a feature that attracts buyers from throughout the world. During the time of the horse show there are also industrial displays and a flower show. There are parties going on constantly in all the town's hotels and it is almost impossible to get accommodations.

There are few countries—if any—where fox hunting is more admired. There are eighty-five active hunt packs. When someone speaks of hunting in Ireland, he is referring only to the pursuit of a fox or a stag on horseback with the aid of dogs. Any hunting that involves the use of guns is called shooting.

Unlike most other countries where fox hunting is the exclusive recreation of the very wealthy, in Ireland those who hunt come from all levels of the population. The season runs from November to mid-April.

Motor Racing

Since it opened in May, 1968, the new Irish motor-racing track of Mondello has been more successful than its planners had dared hope. The season opens on St. Patrick's Day, the seventeenth of March; during the 1969 season, seventeen important car and motorcycle races were scheduled.

This is the supreme goal of all racers in Ireland and is decided on a series of sprints, races, and hill-climbs held throughout the country, mainly on roads that are temporarily closed to the public.

The fast, flat roads of Dublin's vast Phoenix Park are also used once a year for a two-day festival of speed. Racing is growing in Ireland and will probably continue to gain in popularity.

The impulse to gamble appears to have deep roots in the Irish character, and the average Irishman's eagerness to take such risks is a well-known part of Irish life. Betting is open and legal in Ireland, and bookmakers—called turf accountants—have numerous offices throughout the country. Raffles and lotteries are extremely popular. But the horse and dog races, which are held during most of the year, are by far the most popular form of gambling.

Anyone familiar with Ireland and its people would probably agree that the possibility of winning money to spend on things plays a very small part in the Irishman's love of a good gamble; the explanation—if there is any *one* explanation—is certainly far more subtle. If anything, such gambling only emphasizes his disdain for money and material things. By gambling he confronts chance, perhaps unknown forces both within himself and without. The question is open to much conjecture, and it is certainly a fascinating one for sociologists, psychologists, and all students of human nature.

Motorcyclists round a corner during a race through Portstewart in Londonderry

The Gaelic Heritage

Written and oral traditions have undergone many vicissitudes in Ireland; bursts of creativity have been followed by long dormant periods during which little was produced. Generally these are attributed to the centuries of English occupation, which demoralized and disorganized national spirit. Then, during the turn of the nineteenth century, as Ireland's political aspirations were awakened, a bright new surge of creative activity in literature and the theater began to develop. A term often used to describe this is the "Irish Renaissance."

The arts have always been used to promote political and personal ends. In the past, the royalty of Europe "advertised" themselves through portraits of the rulers and their families, which reminded their subjects of their position, power, and elegance. They also commissioned poets to write enthusiastically about their lives and accomplishments. Now, too, the arts were called upon to provide a rallying point for Irish unity and to nourish the flagging Irish spirit.

When thoughtful Irishmen realized that their political maneuvers for independence did not have enough popular support, they turned to the almost forgotten glories of the Irish past.

Before the time of the English invasion in the twelfth century, Gaelic culture was one of the most advanced and richest in Europe. It was particularly noted for the high degree of achievement reached by the tribal bard, or storyteller.

T. P. McKenna, Abbey Theatre actor, relaxes with friends backstage after a performance in Dublin

Now Irishmen returned to this old tradition and worked in many ways to revive it. One of the spearheads of this movement was the Gaelic League, an organization founded in 1893 by Douglas Hyde, which sought to restore Gaelic as the official language of Ireland. When, mainly through William Butler Yeats's efforts, the Abbey Theatre opened its doors in 1904, it provided a focal point that drew most of the new Irish playwrights.

At the time of these two major developments, many writers were working in poetic and prose forms. Among the most famous were George Russell (usually referred to as A.E.), John M. Synge, Sean O'Casey, George Bernard Shaw, James Joyce, Samuel Beckett, and (somewhat later) Seán O'Faoláin, Frank O'Connor, and Brendan Behan. But there was one man whose reputation reaches back to the past century, whose fame continued to grow until his death in the late 1930's and has still increased since then—the playwright and poet William Butler Yeats.

William Butler Yeats (1865–1939)

Yeats was deeply concerned with three main goals: the creation of a new philosophy, a new form of literature, and the rebirth of Irish nationalism. Each, in Yeats's mind, was closely bound up with the others. He saw Irish folklore, for example, as the expression of ancient philosophic concepts. According to William Irwin Thompson, Yeats "saw the peasant as the preserver of an ancient and mystical world view, a world view that had been obliterated as life had become more deliberate abstract and complex. In this folklore he saw a way of bringing together his three passions for the national, the pastoral, and the mystical."

Yeats wanted to escape the vulgarity of Victorian culture and hoped for a return to mythology and magic. He studied the miracle and mystery plays of the medieval period and tried to find ways to revitalize contemporary theater with an essential otherworldliness. Detesting commonplace journalism and everyday jargon, he explored peasant speech.

When Yeats was a young man, scholars had just begun to redis-

Sean O'Casey wrote numerous plays for the Abbey Theatre: Juno and the Paycock, The Plough and the Stars, *and others*

William Butler Yeats

cover the richness of Gaelic literature which had largely been forgotten. The Irish Texts Society was founded by some of these scholars to collect and edit early manuscripts; Yeats and his friends established the Irish Literary Society, whose members had as their object the appreciation and critical study of Gaelic literature.

Much of Yeats's life was spent in County Sligo, which today has an annual Yeat's Festival and where one can take detailed tours of what has come to be called "Yeats Country." Drumcliff Abbey, just a short drive from the town of Sligo, is one of the most important sites for Yeats admirers, for here, in the graveyard where his great-grandfather had been rector, the poet is buried. He lies in Drumcliff churchyard in accordance with his last wishes, under a stone that bears the last lines of the epitaph he himself wrote:

> Under bare Ben Bulben's head
> In Drumcliff churchyard Yeats is laid.
> An ancestor was rector there
> Long years ago, a church stands near
> By the road an ancient cross.
> No marble, no conventional phrase;
> On limestone quarried near the spot

Frank O'Connor

By command these words are cut:
Cast a cold eye
On life, on death.
Horseman, pass by!

Frank O'Connor has written:

> Yeats was famous for studiously creating a vanishing effect. Tall,
> with thick, soft grey hair finely rumpled, a dandy with negligence
> in collar and tie with the black ribbon dangling from the glasses
> on a short, pale, and prescient nose—not long enough to be Roman,
> not sharp enough to be beak, he came to meet one, a big ring on
> his finger. But the nearer he got the further way he seemed to float.
> His air was bird-like, suggesting at once one of the notable swans
> of Coole and an exalted blindness.

Like most famous writers, Yeats was not averse to helping himself
to an occasional line from another man's work. George Moore was
referring to this when he would say, "Yeats has got off with the
spoons." Once Yeats told Frank O'Connor as he came to dinner,
"O'Connor, I've stolen another poem from you." O'Connor asked,
"Did you make a good job of it?" to which Yeats replied with delight,
"I made a *beautiful* job of it."

Yeats's sense of wit and love of the dramatic came to the fore
during the many years he spent in the theater. For those who know
its history it is almost impossible to think of the famous Abbey
Theatre without Yeats's name coming to mind.

The Abbey Theatre

William Butler Yeats was the man with the vision and determination
to found the Irish Literary Theatre in Dublin. But it was an English
woman, Miss Annie Horniman, who made Yeats's dream become
reality by buying and adapting the building that was to become known
as the famous Abbey Theatre. Annie Horniman's generosity was partly
a gesture of her deep admiration for Yeats, but it was also caused by
her own feeling for Ireland.

Under Yeats and Lady Gregory (Irish writer and patron of the arts), the Abbey did not overly concern itself with political issues, but it definitely contributed to the burgeoning nationalism that developed into the insurrection of 1916. After the new Irish government came into being, it granted a small subsidy to the Abbey, which has been increased constantly until the present day. Although government support of this type does not seem particularly unusual today, it was a history-making gesture, for prior to this time, no theater presenting plays in English had been given a state subsidy in any part of the world.

The original Abbey Theatre was destroyed by fire in July of 1951. After many difficulties and delays, a handsome new building was dedicated in July of 1966. Later a smaller theater was constructed under the main building, called the Peacock Theatre. This is where the Abbey produces experimental plays with small casts, or those in poetry or the Irish language.

On January 26, 1907, the Abbey staged the first production of J. M. Synge's *The Playboy of the Western World*. The result was a theater riot, the first—but by no means the last—in the history of the famous Abbey Theatre.

One of the reasons for the outbreak of disorder was the mention of the word "shift" (meaning a female undergarment). That the audience could become so inflamed about this word reveals much about the prudery and taboos of the period. The stage carpenter commented, "Isn't Mr. Synge the bloody old snot to write such a play!"

But there were other reasons why the audience was provoked. *The Playboy of the Western World* is about a young man who seeks refuge in the west of Ireland, in the belief that he has committed a crime. A certain amount of romantic interest is introduced, and among the women who become interested in this young man is a bold widow who tries to get him to hide in her cottage. By modern standards, the story is tender, gentle, and very old-fashioned, but Irish audiences at the turn of the century considered it an insult and outrage to the Irish people. They shouted, booed, hissed, and stamped their feet. The management sent for the police, arrests were made, and the management was prosecuted.

Lady Gregory (1852–1932), playwright and one of the founders of the Abbey Theatre

The riots continued for a week. People were deliberately sent to the theater by various political clubs to cause uproars that would make the play inaudible. Lady Gregory brought in some undergraduates from Trinity University to support the performance, but they made matters worse by singing "God Save the King." Almost unbelievably, from our vantage point in history, the critics agreed with the narrow-minded audiences. The play was described by one as "calumny gone raving mad." Another said it was an "unmitigated, protracted libel . . . a hideous caricature."

William Butler Yeats, the theater director, was called to the police court, where the following interrogation took place:

Magistrate (Mr. Mahony): Did you read this play, Mr. Yeats?

Y: Yes—and passed it.

M: Is it a caricature of the Irish people?

Y: It is no more a caricature of the people of Ireland than *Macbeth* is a caricature of the people of Scotland or *Falstaff* a caricature of the people of England.

M: Is the play typical of the Irish people?

Y: No, it is an exaggeration.

M: Then you will admit it is a caricature?

Y: An exaggeration.

M: Thank you Mr. Yeats. . . . The prisoner will be fined forty shillings and with the alternative of one month's imprisonment and to find sureties in ten pounds for his future behavior.

Although the theater director had taken what would seem to be a sufficiently hard line, demands for the play's withdrawal continued. Yeats declared that neither the house nor the race that bred him had given him a pliant knee, and he was not going to bend before the public. But he agreed to open the theater for a general discussion once the play's run had been completed.

On the night of the discussion, the streets leading to the Abbey Theatre were teeming with police, who moved among the obviously agitated crowds of antagonists and admirers. The group that assembled in the theater was menacing and vociferous, but Yeats answered their objections masterfully. When accused of being an anti-Irish propagandist, he replied, "It is the author of *Cathleen ni Houlihan* [a fervently Irish play] who addresses you," and the audience realized that it could not with any real justification question Yeats's allegiance to Ireland.

The Abbey's main business is to foster the growth of Irish drama by focusing on new plays by native authors, but the theater's presentations are not by any means limited to Irish works. Guest artists and directors from many countries are invited to participate in new productions by foreign writers.

The availability of a permanent company of trained and talented players is of great benefit to dramatists. Because of the Abbey's policy of constantly putting on new, untried plays, many of them unknown, or by little-known authors, the dramatist has an excellent chance that his work will receive a highly polished performance by skilled professionals.

The existence of a permanent repertory company such as the Abbey is essential for the development of young actors, actresses, and directors. Since so many different plays are put on in the Abbey and players are called upon to take on a number of differing or contrasting roles, the various aspects of their talents have a good chance to develop.

The work of the permanent company gives discriminating playgoers a theatrical experience they could not get if productions were put on, however brilliantly, with casts especially assembled for each play. It enables audiences to watch the progress of rising actors as they move from role to role and to understand the virtuosity necessary in a truly mature actor.

Furthermore, when players act together for years, each in a wide variety of parts, their performances will have more natural spontaneity and cohesion than usually can be expected from a type-cast group whose members are unused to working with each other.

Jonathan Swift (1667–1745)

The son of an Englishman who had settled in Ireland, Jonathan Swift is best known as the author of *Gulliver's Travels*. Born in Dublin, he was educated at Kilkenny Grammar School and Trinity College, Dublin. After his rise to fame he enjoyed great political as well as literary influence. He was the intimate friend of ministers of state, who often asked his advice. The nobility sought his favor in England. After his *A Tale of a Tub*, which satirized clerical fanatics and corrupt politicians, opposition to the writer began to build up. Swift returned to Ireland and remained there the rest of his life, although he regarded it as a place of exile. In Dublin he became active in political matters and attacked British politics in many inflammatory pamphlets. He also printed scathing attacks on the rapacity and irresponsibility of English landlords and advocated a tax on absentee landlords.

Swift's masterpiece *Gulliver's Travels,* planned in 1711, was written mainly in Dublin. It was published in London in 1726. Its great attraction is that it can be read on two levels—as a children's book as well as a pungent and meaningful adult satire. Its Lilliputians and Yahoos, its warmongers and mad scientists, its flying island, which is used to flatten disobedient cities—all have their counterparts in the

Oscar Wilde in 1892

world of today. Like all great satirists, Swift had a positive sense of values:

> His satire points at no defect
> But what all mortals may correct;
> For he abhorred the senseless tribe
> Who call it humour when they jibe. . . .

(From satirical verses written on the occasion of the death of Dr. Swift.)

There is a bust of Dean Swift near his grave in St. Patrick's Cathedral, where he preached, and the epitaph he wrote for himself:

> Here lies Jonathan Swift
> For thirty years Dean of this Cathedral
> Where savage indignation
> Can no longer rend his heart.
> Go, traveler,
> And imitate if you can
> This stout champion of human liberty.

Oscar Wilde (1854–1900)

Oscar Fingal O'Flahertie Wills Wilde was born in Dublin, and he died in Paris after a life of great tragedy. Of prosperous parents, he went to Oxford and became a well-known and much admired playwright and poet (*The Importance of Being Earnest, Lady Windermere's Fan*). Then he began to flaunt his aesthetic ideals, which were as eccentric in their way as the pompous, rigid conventional ideas he opposed. His downfall came when he was convicted on a morals charge and sentenced to imprisonment. Out of these experiences came two of his most important works, *The Ballad of Reading Goal* and *De Profundis*. Needless to say, Oscar Wilde is also on the Irish list of proscribed authors.

George Bernard Shaw (1856–1950)

G.B.S.—as Shaw was known through most of his long career—was a social reformer as well as a dramatist. His plays were written not only to amuse but to instruct audiences that were, in Shaw's view, ignorant of the merits of socialism.

George Bernard Shaw

He had written five unsuccessful novels before he became a drama critic; finally, after turning to the theater in hopes of finding the best medium for his talents and the dissemination of his ideas, he wrote a number of plays that made him famous throughout the world. *John Bull's Other Island* was written at the request of W. B. Yeats for the Irish theater. This and other great plays, such as *Major Barbara, Man and Superman,* and *Pygmalion* (later to become the famous musical play and film *My Fair Lady*) won Shaw the Nobel Prize for literature in 1925.

Shaw was as articulate verbally as he was with the written word. His iconoclastic wit and pungent observations delighted, and still delight, millions of readers and theatergoers everywhere. Although Shaw was Irish, he preferred to live in England, where he died at the age of ninety-four. Like most other Irish writers of his generation, he found the

James Joyce wrote of the park in Dublin, "St. Stephen's . . . My Green." Although most of his life was spent in exile, Dublin was his city

Ireland of his time much too restrictively Victorian for his taste. And as a Freethinker, he found the Catholic atmosphere oppressive. Yet, expatriate though he was, G.B.S. is unquestionably an important part of the great Irish literary tradition.

James Joyce (1882–1941)

Regarded as one of the greatest writers of the twentieth century, James Joyce was born in Dublin. He was the eldest of a poor family of ten children but received a good education at the Jesuit schools. Very soon his rebellious nature spoke out against his family, the Catholic religion, and Irish nationalism. In his first, mainly autobiographical, novel, *A Portrait of the Artist as a Young Man,* he wrote, "I will not serve that in which I no longer believe whether it calls itself my home, my fatherland, or my church; and I will try to express myself in some mode of life or art as freely as I can, using for my defense the only arms I allow myself to use—silence, exile and cunning." They are a young man's words, but he meant them seriously and spent the rest of his life in self-imposed exile in Trieste, Rome, Zurich, and Paris.

Joyce fled from Ireland in 1904, with a Dublin chambermaid named Nora Barnacle. (They met on June 16, 1904, the day on which the entire action of his novel *Ulysses* takes place.) Because Joyce was opposed to religion, they were not married until many years later. Joyce taught English to make a living, but suffered from constantly deteriorating eyesight. In 1922, *Ulysses* was published by Sylvia Beach, an American woman who ran a bookshop in Paris called Shakespeare and Co., and who was the friend and financial backer of many writers. In *Ulysses,* Joyce developed the interior-monologue and stream-of-conciousness techniques, which many critics believe to be his major contributions to literature.

For several years, the book was considered obscene, and therefore was banned in many countries. (Its sale is still illegal in Ireland; Joyce is on the official list of forbidden authors.) Finally, however, *Ulysses* found its way into the hands of international critics who recognized the work's originality; during the final years of his life, *Ulysses* brought Joyce worldwide fame.

Samuel Beckett (1906–)

Expatriate Samuel Beckett is probably the most famous living Irish writer. In December, 1969, he was awarded the Nobel Prize for literature (which is accompanied by a cash prize of $73,000). Samuel Beckett, the son of a Protestant middle-class family, was educated at Portor Royal, the same school Oscar Wilde attended. He studied at Trinity College in Dublin, and then spent several years traveling in Europe, writing and working in different places, until finally settling in Paris. Except for brief visits, he has not lived in the land of his birth since 1932.

James Joyce is sometimes called Beckett's patron. A frequent guest in the Joyce household in Paris, Beckett knew many of the intelligentsia during the 1930's. Although he wrote constantly during this period, recognition did not come until after the Second World War, when his play *Waiting for Godot* became world-famous.

Beckett's plays have often been associated with the Theater of the Absurd. For many, his voice, which speaks of the absurdity, hopelessness, and meaninglessness of the human condition, expresses the obsessive fears of contemporary man. Man persists, Beckett tells us, but he is chained to boredom. He endures, but he does not know why.

Few critics have found anything very Irish about the art of Samuel Beckett. However, for others, his writings seem to be still another expression of the old Irish impatience with the material limitations of human existence—and of the belief that some profound truth or meaning in life must eventually be discovered.

Beckett's work, like that of most living expatriate Irish writers, is banned in Ireland. It is a source of much controversy both inside and out of the country.

Censorship

No article, book, or conversation about the arts in Ireland can avoid touching on the censorship laws, which have been in force since Ireland became a nation. Celebrating the banning of his autobiographical play *Borstal Boy,* the late Brendan Behan wrote (he would chant it to the tune of "McNamara's Band"):

> Oh, me name is Brendan Behan, I'm the latest of the banned,
> Although we're small in number, we're the best banned in the land,
> We're read at wakes and weddin's and in every parish hall,
> And under lib'ry counters you will find us one and all. . . .

Censorship is of the utmost concern not only to writers and readers throughout the world but to anyone who cares for human freedom and dignity. In Ireland, films, books, and periodicals come under the censorship laws; plays, because they are seen by such a small part of the public, do not.

Books are usually banned a month or two after they have been put on sale; this is thought to be ample time for those who want to buy them or order them at the bookshop. Even after a book has been banned,

The distinguished Irish journalist J. P. Murray

a copy may be imported for private use if the buyer can prove that the book is essential to his work or studies.

Advocates of censorship point to these loopholes, saying that anyone who really wants a book can get it and that there is no reason for the entire nation to be exposed to bad or pornographic books.

This begs the question, because it is only the rare individual who is constantly alert to what books are being published and places his order immediately. The bother with the red tape connected with importing a banned book requires time and money few people have. The result is that there are many thousands of books that Irishmen do not even know exist. Many enlightened Irishmen are convinced that this situation creates insularity, and restricts intellectual growth. One Irish journalist has cried out that it "is a crime against every man's right to knowledge and understanding of the people and world around him."

At this point it may be argued that a vast number of books are rubbish and a waste of time and effort that may be put to better use. This is true. But if such high standard is to be reached for, then surely it should follow that the amount of time and money the Irish spend on liquor and gambling could also be diverted to other, productive pursuits.

The first book to be banned was *Point Counter Point,* by Aldous Huxley, in 1930. The almost unbelievable list of authors who were or still are banned include George Bernard Shaw, Frank O'Connor, F. Scott Fitzgerald, Somerset Maugham, Graham Greene, Voltaire, and a great many other prominent names.

Noteworthy to people concerned with the population explosion is a section of the Censorship of Publications Act (passed in 1929), which was introduced by Fitzgerald Kenney, who then told the Dáil, "We will not allow, so far as it lies within us to prevent it, any free discussion on birth control, which entails, on the one side, its advocacy."

In Eamon de Valera's Constitution of 1937, the Censorship Act was given clearer form. Today anyone in Ireland who believes that a book is objectionable may send it, after having marked the offending passages, to the Censorship Board. If the permanent secretary of the board feels there is just reason for evaluating the book, it is then sent to each of the five board members. If three of the five are in favor of banning the book, it is automatically banned. Theoretically, a book cannot be banned simply because it attacks the Catholic Church.

Although it receives far less attention, film censorship is practiced just as rigidly by the Irish authorities. For fifty years it has been the law that a certificate from the film censor be issued for every film shown to the public.

Because most of the people are not aware of how easily films may be cut, much of the editing passes unnoticed. Occasionally, however, sections of a movie become so meaningless that the casual filmgoer wonders what kind of idiot conceived such a film. People who are interested in the art of the film are usually aware of such cutting and deeply resent it.

Enlightened Irishmen are convinced that intellectual curiosity and growth cannot be maintained if censorship is permitted to continue. At the moment their chances of getting the authorities to change their views on the matter are still dim; however, being good Irishmen, one can be sure that their struggle for true intellectual freedom will continue.

Oral Traditions

Until the middle of the nineteenth century, Ireland possessed an unusually rich popular-song literature, a fact on which many visitors to the country commented. The French scholar Joseph Vendryes wrote of this tradition: "It is of special importance, due, first to its natural beauty which makes the songs well worth the attention of any music lover. They have a freshness and spontaneity of feeling, and a delicacy and exactness of expression which rank them beside the most touching creations of this art." Voltaire also remarked on the melancholy quality of these songs and compared them to the French popular songs of the eighteenth century, which express little joy or gaiety.

Frank O'Connor believes there has always been an obsession with the oral tradition in Ireland. He writes, "Because of this the Irish professional classes aimed at producing not the man with the best brain but the man with the best memory. This attitude persisted into our own time, and in every Irish-speaking community there was

Tony Lynch, a famous storyteller who spends part of his time at Bunratty Folk Park

usually someone capable of fabulous feats of memory. A Kerry fisherman recited the three-hundred-odd lines of 'The Lament for Art O'Leary' to D. A. Binchy, though he had heard it only twice in his life, and my old friend Timothy Buckley . . . could recite stories and poems by the hour without once halting for a word." A good example of the eighteenth-century ballad is "Barney Brallaghan":

> 'Twas on a frosty night, at two o'clock in the morning,
> An Irish lad so tight, all wind and weather scorning,
> At Judy Callaghan's door, sitting upon the palings,
> His love tale did pour, and this was part of his wailings:

> Chorus
> Only say you'd have Mister Brallaghan
> Don't say nay, charming Judy Callaghan.

> Oh, list to what I say, charms you've got like Venus,
> Own your love you may, there's only the wall between us;
> You lay fast asleep, snug in bed and snoring,
> Round the house I creep, your hard heart imploring:

136

I've got nine pigs and a sow, I've got a stye to sleep them,
A calf and a brindle cow, I've got a cabin to keep them;
Sunday hose and coat, an old gray mare to ride on,
Saddle and bridle to boot, which you may ride astride on:

I've got an old Tom cat, although one eye is staring,
I've got a Sunday hat, a little the worse for wearing;
I've got some gooseberry wine, the trees have got no riper on,
I've got a fiddle so fine, which only wants a piper on:

I've got an acre of ground, I've got it set with praties
I've got a backey a pound, and got some tea for the ladies
I've got the ring to wed, some whiskey to make us gaily
A mattress and feather bed, and a handsome new shillelah.

You've got a charming eye, you've got some spelling and reading
You've got and so have I, a taste for genteel breeding
You're rich and fair and young, as everyone is knowing
You've got a decent tongue when'er 'tis set a-going

For a wife till death I am willing to take ye
But, och! I waste my breath, the devil himself can't wake ye;
'Tis just beginning to rain, so I'll get under cover
I'll come tomorrow again and be your constant lover.

The Supernatural

The Irish have a good deal of respect for the supernatural; the country
is a treasure trove for anyone who likes ghost stories; the frequency
with which a mention of ghosts enters the conversation will probably
surprise the visitor who is unprepared for this aspect of Irish life.

Another strong interest of the country people is a form of magic that
employs the *pishogue,* a sheaf of rotted grain or a quantity of rotten
meat and eggs. It is considered a reliable way to bring bad luck to an
enemy. To accomplish this, the *pishogue* is buried in the person's land
while a curse is recited; it is believed that as the pishogue rots in the
ground, the accursed person will also rot or wither away.

Cats are not popular in Ireland. Often the aversion to cats is not
articulated, but there is a general feeling that they are regarded as an
incarnation of evil.

The cursing of stones is another bit of magic that still survives. Of
particular interest are forty rounded stones on the island of Inish-

murray, off the coast of Sligo. It is said that by turning the stones contrary to the course of the sun, a person may invoke a disaster upon someone who has wronged him. Other stones throughout the country are believed to have similar powers.

Fairies

In his book *Irish Folk Custom and Belief,* Sean O'Sullivan writes, "It is when we come to the fairies that we confront a belief which is perhaps as old as man himself, and which is still strong even in our own day in rural areas." He believes that the existence of the fairy world helped to solve, in a kind of sensible way, problems that were beyond explanation in a rational manner.

For a large majority of the Irish in the past, the fairies were a real force. They were called The Good People, The Little People, The Noble People, The People of the Hills, The People Outside Us, and other names as well. Generally the Irish do not destroy houses that are no longer habitable but let time and weather turn them into complete ruins. These abandoned houses, called *lisses,* were believed to be the homes of the fairies—as well as the moats, hills, and certain other places that were thought to appeal to them.

Their origin was ascribed to the fall of the angels from Heaven when Lucifer rebelled against God. After St. Michael appealed to God not to empty Heaven entirely, He relented by allowing the angels—fallen or otherwise—to remain where they were. Those who had come to earth could stay there; they became the fairies. It was believed that the fairies that were still falling at the time of the heavenly decree were forced to live in the air.

For the most part, fairies were thought to have a human appearance and also to be of human size. The tiny leprechaun shoemaker, whom we have come to believe a typical fairy, was in fact a unique figure among the fairies.

Fairies were thought to live lives much like those of human beings—working, eating, and even smoking and drinking as humanity does. Like human beings, they could also be mischievous and vindictive.

Since they could be harmful as well as helpful, they were often feared.

138

Certain human beings (and it was thought that some fairy enterprises could be carried out only with human help) were thought to be their associates, and such men or women were regarded with awe and respect.

When the subject of fairies arises today, the modern Irishmen sometimes subtly conveys the idea that if it will give his visitor pleasure and amusement, he will indulge him with stories about fairies, but that he regards them as no more than fanciful folklore. However, in the country such beliefs die hard, and you can still come across blackberry bushes in the fields (thought to be a special favorite for the fairies) that the farmer has been careful to plow around. William Butler Yeats has said, "Our Irish fairy terrors have about them something of make-believe . . . when a peasant strays into an enchanted hovel, and is made to turn a corpse all night on a spit before the fire, we do not feel anxious; we know he will wake in the midst of a green field, the dew on his old coat."

Irish Art

Although the reasons can be only rather vague suppositions, the Irish have never been very much interested in, or developers of, the visual arts. Some writers believe the oral and literary traditions were so strong that energies that might have been channeled into the other arts remained focused on poetry, speech, and other literary forms.

Christianity and art are closely involved in the story of Irish art, but the earliest examples are pre-Christian. At Newgrange, near the town of Drogheda (sometimes called one of the wonders of the prehistoric world), the passages to the tombs are lined with great stone slabs decorated with curious patterns of snakelike figures, circles, and geometric designs. These are believed to have been chiseled sometime between 3000 and 1000 B.C.

When the Celts came to Ireland, they brought their highly developed metalwork skills with them. They mainly used bronze which, in their hands, was worked into jewelry of such beauty that it was exported to England and the continent. Examples of Celtic jewelry—such as the Jeweled Cross of Cong, the famous Tara brooch, and several other important pieces—can be seen in the National Museum in Dublin.

At Kilkenny Design Centre, experts teach the old crafts as art forms

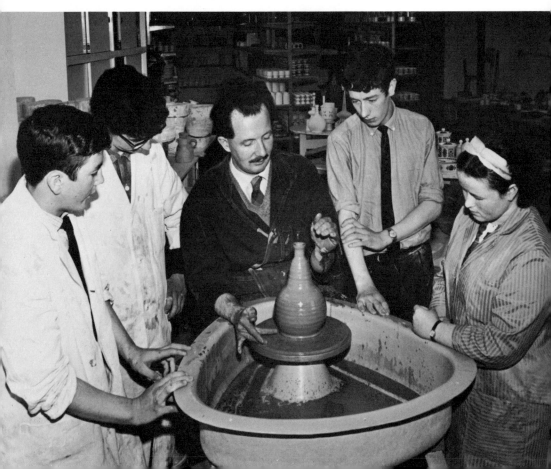

The Book of Kells

Probably the most important work of art in Ireland is the famous *Book of Kells*.

The *Book of Kells*—on view in the library of Trinity College in Dublin—has been called "an inspired, intoxicated dedication to fantasy." It was created in an abbey at Kells in County Meath and is considered the most perfect expression of Christian art that has survived from the Golden Age of Ireland. Like all illuminated (illustrated) manuscripts of this type, it is believed that many monks worked on it. Yet the style never diverges; it appears to have been created by one man.

Liamo de Paro, a Dublin authority on early Christian Irish art, suggests, "If we examine Irish laws contemporary with art of the seventh, eighth and ninth centuries, we will find the same pattern revealed in the mentality of the lawyers, the same love of complexity and intricacy. . . ."

Complexity and intricacy are inadequate words to describe the extraordinary design of this beautiful book. Letters merge into animals, chimerical monsters appear as columns, the simplest, most familiar objects take on a curious, otherworldly character.

The ink used was apparently made from bile obtained from animals, a substance used both in medicine and art. It retains its original blackness to this day. However, it sometimes happened that the ink supplied to the monks who labored over the *Book of Kells* (and other manuscripts) made their work so difficult that they left marginal notes of complaint. One monk wrote in *The Speckled Book,* "Oh Mary Help the ink!" Other notations are such intriguing commentaries on the monastic life as "Thank God I was not in last night," and "Brian is a naughty boy."

After this period of greatness, Irish art fell into a decline from which it has never recovered. Only in recent years have the crafts begun a significant revival. The Kilkenny Design Centre has made great strides in the development of handsome new ceramics, handwoven fabrics, and a great many other things that are not only useful but beautiful. But, interesting as these are, none of them surpass in feeling or design the wonderful handwoven sweaters of the Aran Islanders, which are copied throughout the world.

Aran Fishermen's Sweaters

The traditional Aran stitches each have a meaning; the zigzag stitch was inspired by the crooked mountain paths, the moss stitch by the mossy banks of the islands. The autumn fruits of the bramble suggested the beautiful and widely known blackberry stitch. The honeycomb stitch indicated industry, and the stitch called the tree of life symbolizes the hope of the Aran Islander for many sons. The Islanders' mooring ropes and fishing nets are represented by the cable, diamond, and trellis patterns.

In the past, each family would weave only certain stitches into the sweaters that their men wore. Supposedly, a sailor who died at sea and was unrecognizable when recovered could be identified by the type of sweater he wore.

Funerals

Death in Ireland is an event of great importance. The customs that have evolved concerning the dead have aroused the curiosity and interest of many non-Irish people.

The famous traditional Irish wake, which once involved several nights of drinking, storytelling, eating, and reminiscing is for the most part a thing of the past, although there are still echoes of this tradition in some parts of the country. The Irish are sensitive to the realization that their wakes have become an international joke. Besides, they are far too expensive for the families involved, and, as the Church has admonished, they had become too much of a social occasion.

Now it is customary for the body to remain at home only one night. Then it is taken to the church, where there a brief service and rosary take place the second evening.

The funeral service itself is held on the following morning; it is still a very important event, and the funeral of a prominent member of the community will cause most of the town activities to come to a

142

standstill. The press gives a good deal of space to all funerals, most of it to praise of the departed's morals and his good deeds.

The traditional wake was a merry occasion, particularly if the deceased was an old person. This was by no means simply a desire for festive sociality but, according to many students of folklore, was founded in a deep and universal fear of the dead. Apparently it was thought that the dead were envious of the living, and that they would try to get an opportunity to revenge themselves on those who claimed their property.

Consequently, every effort possible was made to assure the dead that the living still regarded them with sympathy and love. The gay songs and stories, the drinking and dancing were intended to express the respect and honor the survivors felt for the deceased. The dead person was, in fact, the honored guest of the party, and it was hoped that because of the propitiatory gestures, he would acknowledge the kindly feelings of the living. Similar practices have long existed in other parts of the world, and often food, money, weapons, and clothes have been put into the coffin or the burial chamber to accompany the dead into the next world—a custom dating back to the ancient Egyptians.

Why did the Irish maintain the tradition of the wake long after other European nations had given it up? As always, there are many explanations. Certainly one contributing factor was Ireland's oppression— the bitter yoke that kept her from outgrowing such ancient customs. Freedom—and with it, enlightenment—has been slow in coming to Ireland.

The Struggle for Freedom

It was not until the late eighteenth century that the concept of a free Irish republic took shape as a definite political objective. In Belfast, in 1791, a secret society was founded, known as the United Irishmen, which aimed at "a brotherhood of affection and a communion of rights and union of power among Irishmen of every religious persuasion."

The dominant figure of the United Irishman was an unusual man known for his charming personality, his visionary humanism, his wit, and his general philosophy of life. Wolfe Tone was a Protestant from Dublin who had been educated at Trinity College and was keenly aware of the great changes society was undergoing on the continent—the most important being the French Revolution.

Tone had gone to France and seen what the French had accomplished. In Paris he had requested the help of an expeditionary force while forging, at home, a unique alliance between the industrialists and the intellectuals, who found that they could meet and join forces in the name of Irish freedom.

Although Tone managed to raise his troops, his force was too small and his action badly timed. A rebellion that had erupted in Wexford in 1798 was promptly crushed by the British. It was not until 1803 that another Protestant—Robert Emmet—attempted to capture Dublin Castle and set up the Irish Republic. This attempt also ended in defeat. Emmet and seventeen conspirators were captured, tried, and executed.

Trinity College, Dublin, has educated many men like Theobald Wolfe Tone who question the established order

Theobald Wolfe Tone (1763–1798), founder of the society of United Irishmen

The savage attitude of the British was expressed in their handling of the leader; Emmet was first hanged and then beheaded.

The Revolutionary Movement

By 1843, Irishmen were fighting to at least free Ireland from the Act of Union, which had bound her to England in 1800. Daniel O'Connell gave up a brilliant career at the bar to devote his life to Ireland and her emancipation. He organized the Catholic peasantry, attracted the commercial classes, and managed to raise substantial sums of money for the cause of Irish liberty.

O'Connell was a fluent speaker of the Irish language; he had great presence, an extraordinary voice, a sharp wit, and a flair for the dramatic, which his enemies called vulgar. His aims were temperate, for he held a rather romantic admiration for Queen Victoria, whom he called "the darling little Queen." Also his recollection of the horror of the rebellion of 1798, with its hangings, tortures, and floggings, forced him to seek repeal of the Union only by constitutional means. His aim was self-government, not separation from England.

But England was in no mood to tolerate the slightest move toward

146

independence. Reports of the growing fever of insurrection quickly brought fresh troops from England. Before long, the troops stationed in Ireland exeeded the number of troops that were garrisoned in India. "How do you govern it?" demanded Macaulay in the House of Commons on February 12, 1844. ". . . Not by love but by fear . . . not by the confidence of the people in the laws and their attachment to the Constitution but by means of armed men and entrenched camps."

Enlightened, liberal Englishmen continued to speak out against Britain's treatment of Ireland, but they were few and for the most part were ignored. Lord John Russell told the House of Lords in 1846, "We have made Ireland the most degraded and misery-ridden country in the world. All the world is crying in shame upon us."

Thackeray wrote that the history of Ireland

> . . . was a frightful document against ourselves—one of the most melancholy stories in the whole world of insolence, rapine, brutal endless persecution on the part of the English master. . . . There is no crime ever invented by the eastern or western barbarians, no

Daniel O'Connell (1775–1847), known as "the Liberator"

torture of Roman persecutors or Spanish inquisitors, no tyranny of Nero or Alva but can be matched in the history of the English in Ireland.

In 1848, another revolutionary wave swept over Europe. A republican uprising overthrew the monarchy of Louis Philippe in Paris. He quickly sought refuge in London. In Sicily, Venice, Vienna, and other cities of Europe, royalty came to terms with republican liberals or fled for their lives. The revolutionary spark once again caught fire in Ireland, and this time emerged in the shape of a new group called the Young Irelanders. This time an even greater number of professionals, poets, and writers were drawn to the cause of Irish liberty.

Dublin Castle, built in the thirteenth century and formerly the seat of the Irish government, is now a museum

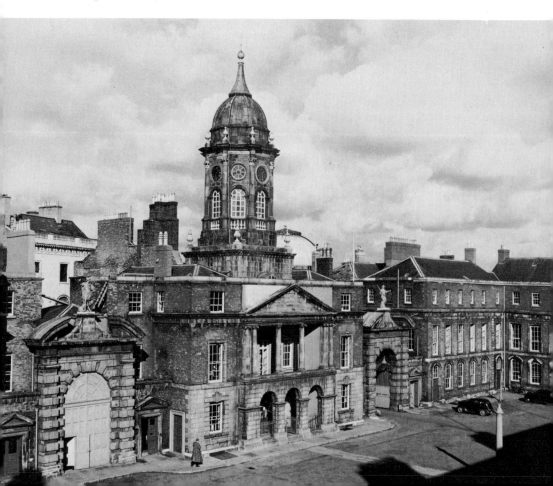

The English were well aware that many parish priests were in sympathy with the Irish peasants. To stop any cooperation the priests might give to the cause, a secret mission was sent to the Vatican, which succeeded in getting a rescript from Pope Pius IX ordering the Irish priesthood immediately to stop all political activity.

By now, of course, the revolutionary movement had gained a momentum that nothing could stop. Many new groups were to form and dissolve before its aims could be achieved; they make a study of Irish history complex and confusing, but always interesting.

The Fenian Brotherhood

In 1858, John O'Mahoney, an Irish emigrant to the United States, formed a secret society he called the Fenian Brotherhood. Its object was of course the same as that of previous secret societies—the liberation of Ireland from British rule. At about the same time, another branch of the movement was established in Dublin. (The Fenians derived their name from the *Fianna* of Irish legend, the ancient military corps who repelled invaders from the Irish coast about A.D. 200.

The first armed uprising organized by the Fenians took place in March, 1867; although quickly suppressed, it succeeded in making the English somewhat aware of the terrible injustices that the British government was perpetrating in Ireland. Prime Minister William Gladstone, leader of the English Liberal party, sponsored legislation that sought to prevent the Protestant State Church in Ireland from demanding tithes from Catholics. Another section of the bill ensured that tenant farmers could retain their rights as long as they were able to pay their rents. These were mainly gestures; they did not begin to alleviate the terrible oppression of the English landowners.

Irishmen continued to grope and dream—and to meet in secret. About 1870, another of Ireland's great leaders appeared from the Protestant Anglo-Irish minority that was to produce so many men in the forefront of liberation. He was Charles Stewart Parnell, the son of an American mother and an Irish father, a typical country gentleman. The young man showed uncommon industry and intelligence; in 1875, at the

Charles Stewart Parnell (1846–1891), statesman and supporter of The Land League

early age of twenty-nine he was elected to the British House of Commons, and three years later he became the head of the Irish Nationalist Party in the British Parliament.

For most Irish, the name Parnell had important associations: Derived from the Gaelic past, it literally means "the Chief." Parnell fought to return the Irish land to Irish ownership and to return to the Irish people their right to legislate for themselves. In doing so, he won the love and devotion of the Irish people.

Working through an organization called The Land League, Parnell tried to help farmers get control of the lands they worked. He encouraged tenants to pay no rent at all unless the landlords reduced it. He advocated the boycott of any tenant who took over the property of an evicted tenant. The word "boycott," meaning to show disapproval by refusing to have anything to do with someone, came into use in 1880. It is derived from Capt. Charles Cunningham Boycott, an infamous English land agent who was hated throughout the countryside because he refused to lower the rents. He was the first person to be boycotted.

Soon the tenant farmers extended the boycott not only to agents but to landlords or to tenants who took over dispossessed property.

Parnell was instrumental in the passage of the Gladstone Act of 1881, which reduced the rents by 20 percent and provided for another reduction in fifteen years.

It appeared that Parnell was destined for even greater events when, very suddenly, he fell into disgrace. It is difficult to conceive of such an uproar, from our vantage point in history, over—a divorce case. Yet that is what happened. Both Prime Minister Gladstone of England and the Roman Catholic bishops of Ireland denounced him, and most of the Irish people turned against him. The blow was too much for Parnell; his health broke and led to his death—at the early age of forty-five in 1891.

The Sinn Fein Movement

Arthur Griffith was a journalist who in 1899 founded an organization called Sinn Fein, which means "We Ourselves." Its main objectives were the withdrawal of Irish members from the British Parliament and the creation of organized passive resistance to British rule.

*Arthur Griffith (1872–1922),
journalist and founder of Sinn Fein*

151

Their efforts were gradual, but slowly some results could be seen. In 1903, Parliament passed an act that gave a bonus to landlords who sold land to their tenants. At last there was some impetus to direct the movement of land back into Irish ownership.

Home Rule for the Irish—control over their country's domestic affairs—was another matter. The Tory party in England was firmly opposed to Irish Home Rule; it was supported by predominately Protestant counties in Ulster, who also opposed Home Rule. They feared that independence for Ireland would mean Catholic domination of the entire country, and foresaw grave consequences for the Protestants if this were to happen.

Despite all opposition, in 1914 the Home Rule Act was finally passed, but the Ulster counties were exempted for six years. The Irish had hardly begun to grasp the meaning of these new developments when the outbreak of World War I changed the situation once again. The British government now decreed that Home Rule for Ireland would be suspended until the end of the war.

About 160,000 Irish volunteers enlisted in the British army. Members of the Sinn Fein chose to join the Irish Republican Brotherhood (I.R.B.) and trained for the time when they could actively oppose British rule. In their impatience, they could not wait until the English had concluded their struggle with Germany; plans were laid that led to the famous Easter uprising of 1916. (Although now illegal, the Irish Republican Army has survived as a clandestine force, which occasionally takes action. The Protestants of Northern Ireland claim that it was instrumental in the riots of the 1960's.)

The Easter Uprising

In the twentieth century, the idea of insurrection—as a means of gaining Irish independence—was far from the mind of the average Irishman, who knew that his ancestors had tried to gain freedom again and again and had failed every time. British exploitation had continued through so many centuries that any large-scale, cohesive action seemed out of the question.

The men who were plotting to drive the English from Ireland were a small group, unknown to the average Irishman. Their meetings were kept secret not only because of the enemy but also because—unbelievable as it seemed—many of the countrymen who *did* know of their plans were not sympathetic. These doubters, who scoffed at the Irish dreams and called the rebels "Tinpike Men," believed that their hopes for success were pretentious and unrealistic. But the determination of the plotters remained unshaken, and soon things began to move.

The period between 1916, when the Easter uprising occurred, and 1923, the time of the final cease-fire, is called "the Troubles" in Ireland.

Bank Holiday had dawned beautifully clear and warm. It was one of those lovely spring days that irresistibly draws the Irish people out into the parks and fields—for picnics, and walks, for boating and relaxation, and just simply to bask in the warmth of the sun. The roads were thronged with people carrying picnic baskets and sports equipment to Sandymount Strand and Phoenix Park.

At midmorning, Dublin had become an almost silent city. The clanging of the streetcars seemed louder than usual in the strange stillness. Then, around noon, a determined, grim-looking group of men emerged from Abbey Street, turned into Sackville Street (now O'Connell Street), and moved stealthily in the direction of the main post office building.

At the head of the procession, which was about a hundred and fifty strong, marched three men, one of whom carried a drawn sword. The others carried an odd conglomeration of weapons—shotguns, pistols, pickaxes, clubs. Some of them were dressed in the dark-green uniforms and cocked hats of the Citizen Army, but most of them wore whatever they had.

Slowly following behind the men were a closed cab and two wagons. These were filled with other weapons and ammunition—pikes, sledgehammers, more pickaxes, and homemade bombs, as well as a good supply of food.

When this troop reached the post office, an order was given and the men broke ranks and rushed into the building. Within moments, windowpanes were being smashed, and passersby were startled by the falling and shattering of glass on the sidewalks. The muzzles of guns now appeared in the windows, while several figures could be seen on the roof, where they fumbled with the flagpole. In a few seconds the English Union Jack had been lowered and another flag hoisted in its position—the ancient flag of Ireland, green with a golden harp in the center. Beneath the harp were the words, "Irish Republic." Minutes later, another flag was also flying—the green, white, and orange tricolor that was the standard of the Fenians.

One of the leaders appeared on the steps under the portico and started to read the famous proclamation that began:

"Irishmen and Irishwomen: In the name of God and dead generations from which she receives her old tradition of nationhood, Ireland, through us, summons her children to her flag and strikes for her freedom."

Then more men were pouring from the building, who at once began to construct barricades in the street, using rolls of newsprint, wagons, furniture from the post office, carts, and several new motorcycles, which they had taken from a nearby warehouse. When the barricade was finished, the insurgents installed themselves behind it, fixed their guns in position, and waited.

Shortly after midday, a company of Lancers was sent to subdue the rebels at the General Post Office, but they were quickly scattered by rifle fire coming from the building. Three Lancers were killed and a fourth fatally wounded. The Lancers then called for reinforcements, and soon sporadic rifle fire was heard all over the city.

No one was quite sure what was happening. Some believed that the Germans had landed and that it was they who were firing on the British.

Through the center of the city, barricades were erected, the builders employing streetcars, automobiles, even sacks of sugar or flour—anything that could be utilized. Men took their positions behind these, and as night fell, the sniping continued in a fearful, highly tensed atmosphere. That evening, the British Viceroy made a proclamation that stated unequivocably that "the sternest measures were being taken and would be taken for the prompt suppression of the disturbances."

Returning Dubliners who tried to find their way back into the city late in the afternoon were dismayed to learn that no trains and very few streetcars were in operation. There were rumors of trouble, but no one really knew what had happened. A mood of great curiosity, coupled with anxiety, swept the city. News of isolated incidents fanned the flames of alarm. One man, returning to his home not far from St. Stephen's Green, saw a dead horse on the road in front of the Shelbourne Hotel. There was a rumor that the rebels had taken over the Green. People were drawn to the post office, which was the center of activity. By Tuesday morning, the situation had not changed much, except for the bands of looters who had begun to break store windows and to carry away food, clothing, and whatever else caught their attention. But the British forces were becoming more organized. They had taken over the famous Shelbourne Hotel and were raking the Green with machine-gun fire. Machine-gun posts had been established in various parts of the city. And then, as evening approached, one of the most extraordinary and most significant events of the affair took place.

A prominent Dubliner by the name of Francis Sheehy-Skeffington, a man well known as a humanitarian and pacifist, was arrested by the military while he was on his way home. He was turned over to a British captain called Bowne-Colthurst, who took Sheehy-Skeffington with him—as a hostage—on a raid. Later that night, Bowne-Colthurst arrested two journalists named MacIntyre and Dickson, who apparently had had nothing whatever to do with the uprising. Without any further ado, he forced the three men in the barracks yard and, without any trial or further preliminaries, shot them dead. Later Bowne-Colthurst was judged insane, but the incident influenced many people against the British.

On Wednesday the British gunboat *Helga* began to shell the post office from the Liffey River, and heavier fire also came from the Fire Brigade Tower and the Customs House. But other British troops, just landed and approaching the Mount Street bridge, were. fired on by volunteers on either side of the road. It was at this point that the British received the heaviest casualties of the week. Still, the tide had clearly turned in their favor.

James Connolly and Patrick Pearse were the leaders of the Easter

James Connolly (1870–1916), labor organizer and signer of the Irish Republic Proclamation

Rebellion. Connolly had been wounded twice, although not seriously. On Saturday morning, Pearse called Miss Elizabeth O'Farrell (a Red Cross nurse who had spent the entire week in the post office), gave her a white flag, and ordered her to inform the commander of the British forces that he was ready to negotiate. General Lowe, who was in charge of the British troops, demanded unconditional surrender; at 3:30 P.M. on Saturday afternoon, Pearse met Lowe and handed over his sword. For their part in the Rebellion both Pearse and Connolly were executed by the British.

At once, instructions were sent to the rebel garrisons throughout the city, informing them that the surrender was official. Although several leaders were reluctant to comply, all finally agreed that it was the only course of action. The tricolor was hauled down wherever it had flown, and the Irish Volunteers marched in orderly groups to the Parnell Monument, where they laid down their weapons. Through the

156

afternoon and evening, stragglers came, to bring some of the incredibly ancient guns they had used.

Oddly enough, the majority of the Irish people regarded the entire uprising as an absurd and foolhardy undertaking, a waste of good money and time. In Moor Street, the market women threw vegetables and chamberpots at the insurgents. Mobs came from the terrible slums to smash shop windows and to loot. To some, it seemed disgraceful that "opportunists" had chosen to assert their demands at this time of crisis, when so many Irish and English boys were dying at the front in France.

When the British began to take the rebels to jail, mobs of Irish followed the prisoners, spitting and cursing them. Later, some writers claimed that this was all staged by the British, who wished to create the impression that the Volunteers represented a small section of the Irish people, but this does not appear to be true. When the fighting was over, 60 Volunteers, 130 British, and 260 Irish civilians had been killed. Approximately 3,000 persons were wounded and 179 buildings destroyed, and the damage was counted in the millions.

But all of Ireland had finally awakened from her long sleep, and although the rising itself seemed to have ended in failure, the incident had strengthened the national spirit, which could not be quenched any longer. During the next few years, Dublin was to be the scene of the worst kind of trouble—a kind of guerrilla warfare, in which secret sentences and executions, murder at night and bomb throwing were to become commonplace.

In the six years after the uprising there were times when these outbursts of violence seemed to be only instances of outright gangsterism, and the public, sensing the meaninglessness of much of the brutality, was becoming weary of the whole business. As often happens at such times, the militant mood was not confined to the British as objects of hatred but spilled over among the different Irish factions struggling for control. There was jealousy among the leaders and an increasing coldness and harshness became apparent whenever they were in conflict with the British.

During the Troubles, hardly a week passed without some form of violence; it is believed that during this period thirty-seven houses—some of them very fine Georgian mansions—were destroyed.

O'Connell Street was largely in ruins during this time. Before the rising, it had been one of the finest streets in Europe; now the rubble served as a platform for some of the fanatical women fighters of the time, who exhorted their listeners to further action. Dublin had the distinction of being the first capital city in Europe to be wrecked by war in this century.

Because of the general international situation in 1920, the British were reluctant to take all-out military action. Instead, they recruited ex-soldiers in England who were given uniforms that were half black and half khaki and were promptly nicknamed by the Irish "Black and Tans." Their fighting techniques, along with other British measures of suppression, caused the English *Daily News* in October, 1920, to state: "In all our annals there has been nothing to parallel this record of organized and senseless savagery."

Northern Ireland and the Irish Free State

Prime Minister Lloyd George was determined to find some solution to the growing menace of insurrection. He decided to settle first with the Unionist party in the northeast corner of Ireland, where the people wished to remain under British rule because they did not want to be controlled by the Catholic government in Dublin.

The Government of Ireland Act of 1920 was designed to set up two parliaments with restricted powers—one for the nine counties of Ulster (Northern Ireland); the other for the remaining twenty-six counties (including the northernmost County Donegal). But Sinn Fein refused to cooperate, and the chaos continued. An uneasy truce was signed in July, 1921, and a meeting arranged between Lloyd George and the Irish leaders. When the British offered to give Ireland the status of Canada, with full fiscal powers, Eamon de Valera—one of the leaders of the struggle—refused to sign because of the exclusion of Northern Ireland. But the negotiations nevertheless were concluded, and the Irish Free State finally came into being in December, 1921.

Eamon de Valera (1882–   ),
political leader of the Irish
Free State

Eamon de Valera

De Valera's administration extended for all but six of the twenty-seven years between 1932 and 1959. Eamon de Valera was a determined and unyielding nationalist; when he became head of the government in 1932, his main emphasis was on the building of a strong image of Irish identity and cohesiveness. Naturally, de Valera returned to Ireland's past in his effort to arouse the people to a national awareness. His opponents believed him unrealistic; in their minds, he put too much emphasis on Ireland as a last refuge of Gaelic culture, feeling that the country should protect its isolation and remain apart from the rest of the world.

One of his first moves was to wage an economic war against Britain and to create strong international trade barriers in an effort to discourage imports. De Valera also discouraged foreign investment in Ireland (at a time when it was desperately needed) and tried to build up the lagging and disorganized Irish industry.

Although some new industries arose to fill the needs of Irishmen who could no longer buy as readily from the world market, they were not well organized and were notably inefficient. In spite of strong opposition and faced with cold statistics, De Valera could not and would not face the fact that Ireland, with so little natural resources and hardly any industrialization, could never be self-sustaining in the modern world. But Eamon de Valera was persistent and strong-willed; no possibility of achieving his ends was left disregarded. He even tried to get the Irish to drink milk instead of tea, in an effort to stop imports.

One of his prime objectives was making Gaelic the official language of Ireland. Although it is not spoken anywhere else in the world (except in the Scottish highlands), De Valera insisted upon programs that would revitalize interest in the Gaelic language. But the growth of world trade and prosperity has been due to increasing cooperation among the different governments; a return to Gaelic could only lead, ultimately, to a perpetuation of insularity, which would hinder, not help, Ireland's chances for growth.

De Valera went so far as to say in a public address that the Gaelic language was more important for Ireland than the country's political freedom. It was an important symbol to those who had fought for freedom, and it is easy to understand their belief that the young nation must nourish itself on the continuing of its old traditions.

Yet there was opposition from many forward-looking people who saw the study of Gaelic as a step backward in time, a step that could never help bring Ireland into the modern world. One reader wrote to *The Connaught Tribune,*

> If there was only half as much meetings about jobs for people, the people might be better off. I don't expect any of these Gaelic League people, or whatever they are, care a thawneen [straw] for my three sons, but I care for them and I would rather hear them speak English as they worked in a Galway factory or in a Galway shop than know they could talk Irish to themselves as they worked in an English railway station.

During De Valera's time of power, he slowly worked to renew Ireland's national image in the world community and to cope with the enormous problems that beset any young nation. Economically, the people were forced to endure a difficult period. During this time, as in so many previous decades, emigration continued to draw away Ireland's young people. Thousands went to England to work in defense-plant jobs during World War II. Many other thousands came to the United States, Canada, and Australia.

After De Valera retired from political leadership in 1959 (he was then elected to the nonexecutive Presidency), an aggressive new economic policy was instituted by the new leader of the Fianna Fáil party, Seán Lemass. He invited foreign investment and made continuing efforts to lead Ireland into the international community of nations. This was really the turning point, when the Irish standard of living began to become comparable with that of the rest of Europe.

Government buildings in Dublin fly the red, white, and green flag of the Republic of Ireland

The Two Irelands

Boarded-up shopfronts, broken windows, and barbed-wire barricades were a common sight in Northern Ireland's cities during the last years of the 1960's. At night, the streets were safe only for the people who lived in certain areas. Protestants knew they were inviting violence if they ventured out of Protestant neighborhoods, and Catholics took the same precautions. Young toughs, looking for an excuse for brutality and cruelty, seized any opportunity they could find to attack a member of the hated enemy camp—and to be an enemy in Northern Ireland, one need only to belong to a different religion.

Liberals on both sides are familiar with death threats from reactionaries who do not welcome any lessening of tension. Business, too, has suffered. Both Protestant and Catholic shopkeepers claim that communal boycotts have cost them a quarter of their usual business.

The spectacle of destruction and death, and the numbers of refugees seeking safety in the Republic of Ireland, which horrified the world in 1969, were examples of a particularly violent outburst of hatred; but they were not new to the people of Northern Ireland. A deep religious antagonism has flourished there since the area was "planted" by English and Scottish colonists in the seventeenth century. When the Irish Free State came into being in 1921, and the counties of Northern Ireland remained a part of the United Kingdom, the deep-seated fears and hatreds grew even more intense.

Catholics and Protestants, people from Northern Ireland and the Republic, as well as foreign visitors can be found in the crowd at Puck Fair

During the terrible riots of 1921–1922, a group of Protestant toughs called the Murder Gang would come up the Catholic streets storming into houses and shooting people in their beds. Over four hundred were killed during this outburst. There were more outbreaks of violence in the 1930's.

How did this incredible situation develop? To understand it you must first know something of the government of Northern Ireland and its relation to the United Kingdom.

Northern Ireland

Although it is as much a part of the United Kingdom as Wales or Scotland, Northern Ireland, which is often referred to as Ulster, has a unique status in that it has its own Parliament and a large measure of self-rule. Its six counties are: Antrim, Armagh, Down, Fermanagh, Londonderry, Tyrone, and the boroughs of Belfast and Londonderry.

The Parliament, which sits at Belfast, is concerned with domestic matters only; such questions as defense and international relations are decided by the British Parliament. Northern Ireland elects twelve members to the British House of Commons (four of whom represent the Borough of Belfast).

The chief executive is the Governor, who is the Queen's Representative in Ireland. The Parliament consists of a House of Commons of fifty-two members, who are elected by popular vote. The upper house, or Senate, consists of twenty-six members, who are elected by the House of Commons under the system of proportional representation. A senator may hold office for as long as eight years, and the House of Commons has a maximum life of five years. The Prime Minister of Northern Ireland directs a cabinet of eight ministers, most of whom sit in the House of Commons.

Although theoretically all this makes Northern Ireland's government sound like a parliamentary democracy, in actual fact since 1920 the country has been dominated mainly by one party—the Unionists.

"Unionists" refers to the concept of favoring union with England. An ultraconservative party, it is firmly supported by most workers, who seem to prefer it to the more liberal-oriented Labour party. Opposing

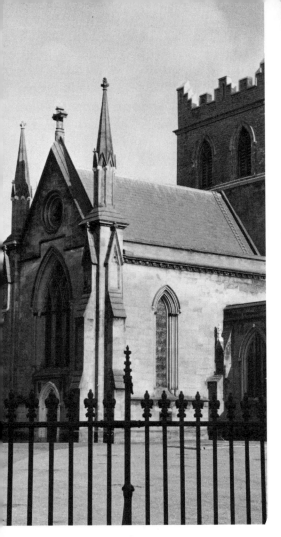

Two cathedrals in Armagh, Northern Ireland. The one on the left is Protestant, the other, Catholic

the Unionists in Parliament are the Catholic Nationalists, whose main concern is to be reunited with the Irish Republic.

Protestant versus Catholic

Two burning issues are causing the deep antagonism in Northern Ireland: religious prejudice and the prevalent economic conditions. There is no doubt that Ulster is far more prosperous than the Republic;

the fact that their standard of living is higher tends to make Ulstermen proud and the men of the Republic envious. In the north, the people attribute their success to their industry and determination. Southerners tend to disagree; they attribute it to British subsidies of £60 million a year.

Although Ulster has only half the population of the Republic, it does twice the trade. Agriculture is more mechanized and accounts for only an eighth of the work force. Medical care is excellent, thanks to the presence of British National Health service. For several years, Ulster has had the highest birth rate and the lowest death rate in the British Isles. It follows that Ulstermen marry earlier (and in larger numbers) than do the inhabitants of the Republic.

Although the Catholics of Northern Ireland share in these benefits, subtle discriminations still exist, which help to keep them on a lower economic level than the Protestants. When a man applies for a job, he is not asked what his religion is but what school he went to. Since all schools are either strictly Catholic or Protestant, the prospective employer knows immediately what the applicant's religion is.

Almost from birth, children are raised in an insular atmosphere, which increasingly marks the ancient division between the two groups. Each religion has its own schools, although the Protestants have often suggested that a union of the two systems would result in great savings and would also reduce the discrimination felt by each side toward the other. The Catholics will not consider this proposal. As one Catholic priest put it, "How could we trust an exclusively Protestant government with the education of Catholic children? They would destroy our community in a generation."

Both school systems now deliberately encourage the polarization of the two groups. Although the state pays more than two thirds of Catholic education costs, Church authorities subtly encourage anti-Protestant behavior. The Protestants, with their vociferous flourishing of the Union Jack, prayers for "our gracious Queen," and other, more provoking demonstrations of allegiance to Britain, reinforce anti-Catholic attitudes.

At home, children are exposed to the unmasked prejudices and hatreds of their parents, so that eventually their thoughts are patterned in the same inflexible mold characteristic of their elders. Although people buy their clothes from the same shops, walk the same downtown streets, and may even work for the same company, the differences separating them are becoming more and more apparent. Catholic submissiveness to the authority of the Church seems to have a mellowing effect on people, resulting in more gentle personalities, greater restraint in speech and manner. There is something here of the mask that is so often seen in the south. By contrast, Protestant speech is harder, more quickly revealing the individual's true feelings. There are even differences in sports. Protestant boys prefer Association football, but the Catholics like Gaelic football—a much rougher Irish version of the game.

When children enter their teens, the gulf between the two groups widens even more. Catholic youths join the Knights of Columbus or the Order of Hibernians, while the Protestants join youth affiliates of the Orange Order, an organization that works to keep alive the spirit of Protestant political life. Orangemen—as its followers are called—are frequently seen in Northern Irish streets, where they seem to derive enormous pleasure from fife-and-drum parades that arouse the martial spirit while proclaiming the Protestant supremacy in the North.

The violent aggression of the Protestants can be traced to their fear: the South is 95 percent Catholic. A union of Northern Ireland with the Republic of Ireland would place the Protestants in a very small minority and would, they believe, lead to discrimination.

A story that illustrates how deep the enmity between the two groups runs is about an American in Belfast who was asked his religion. He said he was an atheist. "Yes," answered the Belfastman, "but are ye a Catholic atheist or a Protestant atheist?"

The terrible thing about the entire situation is that its fierce energies are generated by memories of the past as much as by present-day grievances. In the slums you will sometimes come across freshly painted portraits of William III (of the House of Orange) on the walls. He lived three hundred years ago. Often, splashed in bold printing near by, is slogan "Remember 1690," in memory of that Protestant victory over the Catholics at the Battle of the Boyne. When Catholics talk about Oliver Cromwell's massacre of 3,500 men, women, and children in Drogheda, you have the uneasy feeling that this happened last month or last year, so intense and vociferous are their emotions.

When Northern Ireland was created in 1920, the Catholic minority included within its borders remained emotionally devoted to the ideal of a united, republican, Catholic Ireland. For them, as for those in the South, a divided Ireland was unthinkable, and it was only a question of time until the country would be united. They showed that they would tolerate the division for the time being (the Irish have learned to be patient in such matters), but their actions clearly revealed their attitude toward the Protestants, whose fears of a united Ireland became all the more inflamed.

The Frontier

Throughout the years, the men of the South have been constantly reminded that it is their duty to win back the North—by force, if necessary. From time to time, street-corner meetings take place, with

A street in Fintona, Northern Ireland

A street in Ennis, south of the frontier. The town is very similar to Fintona in the north

banners crying, "Smash Partition!" It is one of the avowed aims of the underground, the illegal force still in existence that is called the Irish Republican Army.

Most Irishmen from the Republic have no desire to go to Ulster. For them it is the "Black North," a place of bigotry, of excessive industry, and rigid Puritanism. No unemployed person from the South would consider going to Ulster to work. To do so, he must have a work permit, and he knows very well that it would not be easy to get one.

Women often do piecework such as hand embroidery in their homes

The frontier that separates the two Irelands is indicative of how the two opposing factions feel about the division. The Republic has erected rather makeshift structures, as if to indicate that the separation is only temporary; sooner or later, they seem to proclaim, *all* of Ireland will be united within the Republic, with Dublin its governmental head.

The northern side of the frontier has solidly constructed buildings. They will endure, the Northern Irish seem to be saying, just as Northern Ireland itself will endure, separate and apart from the feared and hated Catholic South. Tourists traveling from one country to the other must have special entry permits for their cars, and carry an insurance rider.

Once you have passed the frontier, you will find no difference in the landscape but you see quickly enough that many things are different. Policemen are permitted to carry guns, as they do not either in Ireland or England. The roads are better and the farms look more prosperous than in the Republic.

Small, family-owned firms have long been a traditional part of the Northern Irish business scene, especially companies based on the "linen village." Such businesses were begun in small villages because of the local waterpower, and they have flourished there ever since. In most cases, the family that owns the company lives in a beautiful country house, usually built in the eighteenth century. Often, a part of the factory will be situated in the stable yard, with other sections of it located near by. Generally, most of the villagers are employed by this company. Such Protestant strongholds—as this type of business invariably is—quickly reveal the Northern Irishman's attitude toward work.

As with the diligent Scots, who settled Ulster hundreds of years ago, work is regarded as a serious business here. The division between work and play, unlike that in the Republic, is a clear-cut one: When you work, you work hard. You play only during times specifically intended for relaxation and amusement.

Sunday, in the strong Calvinistic tradition of these Protestants, presents a problem because one is not allowed to either work *or* play. Donald S. Connery, in his excellent book, *The Irish,* writes, "If there is a gloomier city in all Europe than Belfast on a Sunday, then I have yet to see it. The pubs close, the cinemas close, many playground swings and roundabouts are chained, and morning church is followed by a long vacuous afternoon."

Belfast

For centuries, Belfast was hardly more than a village; its history was that of the average Irish village—being passed from one owner to another, enduring all the while, the violence that accompanied these exchanges. During the eighteenth century, the city began to grow, but only slowly. Not until the nineteenth century did Belfast become the important, commercial city that it is today.

The two industries that fostered this growth were shipbuilding and linen spinning; they made the city rich, and famous as a busy and prosperous port. Today the great shipbuilding firm of Harland and Wolff is one of the largest in the world.

In Belfast, business and moral traditions are important; aesthetic ones

171

—art, music, theater—are not. The *Belfast Newsletter,* founded in 1737, is still printed in the same place and owned by the same family. During the American Revolution, it incurred English disfavor by upholding the Rebel cause. A good manifestation of Belfast's moral fiber in the past was her staunch refusal to allow slave ships to enter the port—at great financial sacrifice; for this trade simply moved to Liverpool and other English cities, which were to profit from it.

The Belfast accent is different than that of the South. An Englishman noted that while strolling through the streets one evening, he asked a road sweeper the name of a large stone building that he had come upon.

"That is the Monastery," said the man.

Hand-painting china at the Belleek Pottery. This delicate ware is exported to the United States and other countries

The Englishman was surprised. A monastery in the heart of modern Belfast? "But *what* monastery?" he asked. "Cistercian? Benedictine?"

"It is the Monastery of Agriculture," said the man.

In his perceptive book *Ulster,* Hugh Shearman has written,

> The puritan capacity for taking the shortest route from one point to another, for being intense at the point where intensity is required, has produced from among the people of Belfast, and of Ulster generally, some of the world's best engineers, some of the world's most competent administrators, generals, lawyers and men of learning, and the same directness, the same impatience with roundabout ways, is a part of everyday life in Belfast.

Belfast is thought of as a masculine town that has little interest in the arts. And yet it has been acknowledged, even by many literary authorities in the Republic, that the most interesting contemporary literature is being written in the North. Among the best known of the writers, who have now become expatriates are Brian Moore, Brian Friel, and Edna O'Brien. It seems that few people in the North choose a life in the creative arts, but that those who do, put into their careers the same industry and intensity as do their counterparts in business.

Some writers detect feelings of inferiority in the people of Belfast. They are, report these writers, aware that Dublin is more social, more attractive, a more cosmopolitan and amusing city. They are alert to slurs about Belfast and quickly rise to its defense.

Although work is considered good for its own sake, no Ulsterman is disregardful of its rewards. It is said that the Ulsterman loves the Crown, but that he loves the half crown still more. The accumulation of a fortune fascinates the mind of the average young Ulsterman; he is often willing to devote years of his life to boring work in its pursuit. Brian Moore (who was born in Belfast) describes the town as "a dull city where men made money the way charwomen wash floors, dully, alone, at a slow methodical pace."

Londonderry

Catholics often object to the name Londonderry. As England's first colony, it is a constant reminder of Ireland's centuries of subjugation by the English.

Bishops Gate in the famous walls of Derry, with the guildhall in the background. It is possible to walk around the ancient walls

The name came into being in 1613 when the British, as previously mentioned, brought in "planters" as a means of quelling the rebellious Irish. It was the first Protestant colony to face a hostile Catholic Ireland —all the more hostile because the English had expelled Irish landowners in order to have lands for the English planters. The administration of the plantation was given to the Corporation of the City of London, and thus is became literally London's Derry.

Theoretically it is still controlled by the Corporation—an assembly of twenty-six members who call themselves the Honorable The Irish Society. In accord with tradition and their administrative position, they make ceremonial "visitations" to the area every year.

The physical characteristics of the city of Derry reflect the political structure of its society. On the highest point of the city—the top of Bishop Street—are three important buildings that symbolize England's long domination of the city. One of the buildings is a handsome Georgian house that is the local headquarters of the Honorable The Irish Society. The courthouse, nearby, is an impressive building with a Palladian facade that immediately brings to mind imperialist British law. The third building is St. Columba's Cathedral of the Church of Ireland, which is the Irish version of the Protestant Church of England.

In the neighborhood of these important buildings are the prosperous homes of the Protestant community; farther below are the populous Catholic areas. It was here—in 1688–1689—that the Protestants withstood a 105-day Catholic siege, a battle that still brings a thrill of pride to Protestant hearts and a stab of pain to Catholic ones. According to legend, the garrison's commander, General Lundy, had decided to capitulate when thirteen young apprentice boys firmly held the gates shut as they vowed, "No surrender!"

This motto is still frequently heard on Protestant lips in Northern Ireland. "Lundys" is the despicable name given to anyone suspected of betraying the Protestant cause.

Derry has a population of sixty thousand people—two thirds Roman Catholic. They find it intolerable that because of gerrymandering, the town council has always had a two thirds majority of Protestants. This naturally leads to unfortunate economic consequences for the Catholics and deprives them of municipal housing advantages as well. In the municipal offices of Derry, two thirds of the jobs and nearly three quarters of all salaries are given to Protestants.

Although Derry is the second city of Northern Ireland—after Belfast—its unemployment rate is a very large 13 percent. This is twice as high as the rest of the province and is thought to be higher than any other place in Western Europe. Nine out of ten men who do not have work are Catholics, and they are deeply resentful of the Protestant power structure, which they feel is responsible for their situation. "I haven't had an hour's work out of this place for five years," one man in his fifties said. "If there's any job going, it'll go to a Protestant." Other men grumble, "No bloody Protestant will give us a job if there's a chance he can give it to another Prod [slang for Protestant.]" Poor Protestants counter this charge by pointing out that it's a rare Catholic who will give a Protestant a job.

Catholics who are "on the dole" generate greater hostility among the Protestants because of their large families. Their birthrate, like their unemployment rate, is also one of the highest in Europe. Their refusal to consider the Pill infuriates Protestants, who see their taxes being used to pay living expenses for large Catholic families, and they are growing larger all the time.

Recent Reforms

During much of 1968 and 1969, violence was confined to Londonderry; then, as the intensity of feeling on both sides grew, Belfast, too, became involved. The deep mutual hatred and long divisiveness were underscored by parades that commemorated old victories for either the Catholics or the Protestants.

Ironically, throughout much of 1967, a number of reforms made it appear as if Northern Ireland were moving toward a more equitable law. These had been guided through Parliament by Prime Minister Terence O'Neill, who was a firm believer in reform. But in April of 1969, the mounting tensions and violence throughout the country caused his fall; another reformer, Major James Chichester-Clark, became the Prime Minister and pledged sweeping civil rights legislation. He immediately agreed to several reforms on the lines that the Catholics had been demanding.

The government has finally decided to revise the electoral boundaries, which will give Catholics far more power than they have had at any previous time. In Londonderry, the largely Protestant City Council has been disbanded, and replaced with an appointed commission that is representative of both the Catholic and the Protestant communities.

And yet none of these moves, because they have not been fully implemented, have helped the deteriorating situation. The deep mutual resentment and distrust are stronger than ever; moderates on both sides are under constant pressure to revise their views, and, as always in such situations, reactionaries on both sides have gained power and followers.

One important factor that has contributed to the mounting violence is the attitude of the Catholics toward the police, who are predominately Protestant. Catholics feel they cannot trust men who theoretically are responsible for maintaining law and order, but who in practice are as bigoted and biased as their fellow citizens.

The Future

There are times when the problems of Northern Ireland appear insoluble. Intelligent Irishmen, realizing the complexity of the issues, know that nothing will be helped by impetuous and violent measures.

Visitors to Northern Ireland entering from the car ferry at Larne near Belfast. There are many cross-channel boats between Britain and Ireland

But any problem that involves *both* religion and economics is certain to generate dangerous emotions.

Many observers believe that once the economic problems are solved, the religious controversies will gradually die down. In fact, many Catholics openly admit that it is the economic factor which they consider of greatest importance. Although they may be very vocal about their hopes for a united Ireland, even some of the staunchest Catholics will privately state that equal rights—which would automatically lead to better economic conditions—are their main objective.

Countering this, the Protestants deny that inequality exists at all. They see the Catholics as the dupes of Irish extremists who are inflaming the issues to provoke actions which, they hope, will eventually lead to chaos in Northern Ireland and an ultimate union with the Republic.

Enlightened circles on both sides freely admit that anti-Catholic discrimination is undeniable. Some church authorities work closely together to soothe tempers and create a peaceful atmosphere. During one particularly dangerous period, the Catholic Bishop of Derry and three Protestant colleagues toured the city together, appealing for peace. On some nights, when parades were planned for the following morning, both Roman Catholic and Church of Ireland cathedrals have remained open throughout the night for those who wished to pray.

Bernadette Devlin

One of the most interesting Irish political figures to emerge during 1969 was Bernadette Devlin, a student at Queen's University in Belfast. At the age of twenty-two, Miss Devlin became the youngest woman ever to sit in the British House of Commons as a Member of Parliament.

Her startling political career began almost by accident in the autumn of 1968. While on a march from Belfast to Londonderry with hundreds of other students, she witnessed the brutality that can suddenly arise when two opposing groups lose control and the police are called in to restore order.

"My reaction to what I saw was sheer horror," Miss Devlin said, "I could only stand rooted as the police battered and beat, and eventually

178

Bernadette Devlin and fellow rioters in Londonderry after being tear-gassed by British troops. Miss Devlin was sentenced to jail for her part in the riots

I was dragged off by another student who came between me and a police baton. After that I *had* to be committed."

After this experience, she became active in various student groups and worked on committees. Soon her courage, wit, and fiery determination won her the chance to stand in an election to Parliament. During the election, several threats on her life were made, but she was unswerving in her will to win. "I spoke and the people came to listen," she said, "I'd say to the people, *this* is what I believe in, *this* is what I can do, *this* is what we can accomplish if we stand together."

Bernadette Devlin won a tremendous victory in a 92-percent turnout. After her maiden speech in the House, the London *Times* headline said, "Miss Devlin enthralls packed house with straight-from-the-heart speech."

In August, Bernadette Devlin went to the United Nations with her defense of the Roman Catholic cause in Northern Ireland. When she later spoke to a crowd of Irishmen who had gathered to hear her, they roared their approval when she called for a "boycott of all things British." Later on, a policeman traveling with the Devlin party remarked, "Wherever she goes she gathers crowds and she wins them over, Irish and non-Irish." But in Northern Ireland, the chairman of the ruling Unionist parliamentary party was less complimentary about her. He said she was dangerous in that she is a presentable front for activists who would like to destroy Northern Ireland.

That is really at the bottom of all Protestant discrimination—not an active, willful desire to persecute those of another religion but a deep

John Lynch, Prime Minister of the Republic of Ireland in 1969

and abiding fear that any new power the Catholics gain will lead to a resurgence of nationalism and calls for union with the South. They believe that such a union would definitely place the Protestants at an economic disadvantage and—recalling the actions of Catholic toughs during the riots—perhaps even worse.

John (Jack) Lynch, the Prime Minister of Ireland, did not reassure anxious Northern Ireland Protestant groups when he declared, on September 20, 1969, that Ireland's long-term objective was reunification of the whole country.

He suggested that one form this reunification might take would be a federation between North and South. "We have no intention of using force," he said in a speech at Tralee, County Kerry, "but changes there must be. I need not explain or justify the fundamental desire of the over-whelming majority of the people of this island for the restoration in some form of its national unity. This desire is not confined to Irishmen of any particular creed or ancestry. . . . The unity we seek is not something forced but a free and genuine union of those living in Ireland based on mutual respect and tolerance."

Such a union—based on these precepts—would be a wonderful thing for Ireland. And it would also be something of a miracle.

Toward the Mainstream

Change has been slow to come in Ireland, but now it has *come,* and even the most casual visitor to the country can see that many more changes, profounder changes, are just around the corner. Up until the 1970's, the most significant changes have been economic; the living standard of the average Irishman has changed drastically for the better, in the last fifty years.

Although many Irishmen resent the fact, there is no doubt that the country remains connected to England by strong commercial ties. Irish currency is kept on a par with the English pound sterling and was devalued in 1968 (because of extensive trade with Britain) when the English pound was devalued. Most of Ireland's exports are sent to the United Kingdom (Britain and Northern Ireland), and, in return, the majority of Irish imports stem from there. But it is becoming even more apparent to the Irish that the most likely source of increased income is the unique beauty and charm of their country itself. Ireland is fast developing into one of the major tourist-oriented nations of the world.

Tourism

It would be difficult to find a country better suited than Ireland for a young person's first trip abroad. There is no language barrier at all except in the west, where certain accents are hard to understand—and even there it is but a minor problem. Food and accommodations are

A guide for Bunratty Castle tours awaits tourists arriving on Aer Lingus (Irish Airlines) at Shannon Aiport

Jaunting car at Ross Castle, Kilarney. This is a popular way of touring the lakes

cheaper than in most other parts of the world. The pace of life, which allows time for talk, reflection, and poetry, appeals especially to teen-agers, who usually loathe the rat-race existence endured by most urbanites today. Time, spent in leisure, in amusement, in nostalgia and dreaming, the Irish seem to say, is not time wasted. The famous Judeo-Protestant ethics, which associates hard work and material gain with godliness, is noticeably absent in Ireland.

Another important factor that will be useful to any teen-ager whose parents are reluctant to allow him—or her—a trip abroad, is the amazing lack of crime. People of all ages (and this most definitely includes teen-age girls) hitchhike everywhere in the country without fear. Irish hospitality is a living tradition, whether you enter an Irishman's home or his car. He will respect you, he will be courteous, and the chances are he will go quite a bit out of his way to help you on your journey.

The police are known as "the guards"; generally, a policeman is referred to as the *garda* (two policemen are the *gardai*). The majority of them use bicycles or go on foot and they are unarmed except for batons (billy clubs).

Homicide in Ireland is almost nonexistent. The incidence of theft and other crimes is one of the world's lowest. One reason for this low crime rate is the authoritarian structure of society that has existed for so

"Caravans" modeled on the trailers that tinkers live in. These can be rented for a modest fee and are a leisurely way to see the countryside

long and still exists, in Ireland. But, whatever its causes, the extraordinary absence of crime in Ireland is a great comfort for travelers and particularly for young people going abroad for the first time.

An annual event that has been growing increasingly important for young people is the Yeats International Summer School, which is held for two weeks in Sligo every August. For all those interested in poetry, and especially for lovers of W. B. Yeats's work, two extraordinary weeks of literary lectures, seminars, and discussions are offered. Twenty-one lectures are given, such as, for instance, "Yeats and Swedenborg," or "The Poet and the Rebel."

These lectures are held during the day. A very popular attraction during the afternoon are the bus tours of the Yeats country and other parts of western Ireland, which are conducted during class breaks. But at

At the Fleadh Cheoil in County Wexford everyone joins in dancing in the street

night it is often difficult to choose between the various entertainments offered—poetry readings, films, productions of Yeats plays, or informal gatherings at the school's social centers. Many students feel that perhaps the most delightful part of the evening is the folk music sung by young local Irish people, and often by visiting guests from abroad.

To facilitate making the necessary arrangements for such a stay, the Yeats Society Accommodations Committee will be glad to take care of all details, if wished. Youth hostels provide room and board at very inexpensive rates. Several scholarships are granted to American students each year, which cover board, room, and tuition. All the student has to pay is the fare. To be eligible, a student must submit a recommendation from the head of the English Department at his college or university.

Everyone who makes a literary pilgrimage to Ireland will want to see the tower at Ballylee Castle, where W. B. Yeats worked for several years. It is part of a fourteenth-century ruin, which Yeats purchased for a hundred pounds. It is said to look exactly as it did when the great poet and writer lived there.

Festivals

At almost any time of the year in Ireland, you will probably find some festival in progress. When the Waterford International Festival of Light Opera is in season, in September, the streets of the town are full of Welsh tenors singing and drinking. Another song festival—which this being Ireland, also features drinking—is the Cork Choral Festival in May. Cork also has a film festival in September, which is gaining in importance. Dublin also holds its Theatre Festival in September. Less prestigious is the Spring Festival of Opera in Dublin.

One of the most curious festivals held in Ireland is the Puck Fair at Killoglin. It is a strange celebration to find in austere and ascetic Ireland, for it is the goat—ancient symbol of fertility and also of lasciviousness—that is honored. Such fairs, which paid tribute to the goat, were once common in Europe, but for centuries now they have not existed. For all practical purposes, the Puck Fair is just another cattle fair similar to many that are held through the countryside during

Horses are exhibited and traded at Puck Fair in County Kerry. This one is being loaded for the journey home

the year. But there is often more of a carnival atmosphere here; the high point is reached when a goat is crowned King Puck of the fair and enthroned at the top of a tall tower of tubular scaffolding for the three days of the fair. The first is known as the Gathering, the second as Puck, and the third as the Scattering.

Journey to the Arans

There is one journey in Ireland that is certain to revive all tired or flagging spirits after too many days at crowded festivals or in the cities. The Aran Islands—Inishmore, Inishmaan, and Inisheer—are especially attractive to young people who want to seek out places that are removed from the hectic life of our cities.

But even here—as on several other islands near the Irish coast—life patterns are changing. A large number of these islands have been deserted by the people, who found their isolated lives intolerably difficult. On the Aran Islands, the population has declined from over three thousand, about a hundred years ago, to only sixteen hundred people.

Sometimes the reason given for the decline is that fishing, the mainstay of the islands' economy, is not as good as it once was. What is far more likely, though, is the probability that younger people are no longer content to live with the hardships that are an inevitable part of island life in this part of the world.

The trip from Galway, the largest city on Ireland's west coast, to Kilronan, on Inishmore, takes three hours to make the twenty-eight-

Aran Islanders carrying a currach. These traditional fishing boats are made of tarred canvas stretched over a framework of wood

mile journey. (With the end of summer, schedules are cut back; the boat sails only twice a week, and when the weather is bad even those trips are canceled.)

When you arrive, there probably will be men lined up on the dock with their two-wheeled pony traps, or carts, who can be hired to take you on a sight-seeing tour around the nine-mile-long island. These men, like most of the other people living on the islands, usually wear home-spun fabrics. There is little electricity on the island; most people still use gas lamps. The men of Aran still put to sea in their distinctive currachs—canoelike boats made of black-tarred canvas stretched over a wooden frame. This is still the main means of transport between the three islands. Although there are no hotels or formal restaurants, several of the island women will open their houses to paying guests. Their prices are amazingly low both for food and lodging.

The Aran Islands have attracted artists and writers for a long time. Robert Flaherty's great pioneering documentary film *Man of Aran* was made here during the 1930's. It is an event still vividly remembered by some islanders.

Around the turn of the century, John Millington Synge, the Irish dramatist, went to live on Inishmaan, where he wrote the well-known play *Riders to the Sea,* which concerns an island woman who clings fiercely to her life on the island even though her family has lost all of its men to the sea.

Some travelers to the islands report that the inhabitants are becoming aware of how much money tourism can bring in. Hopefully, this will never mar the unique charm and beauty of the Aran Islands.

Blarney Castle

Ireland possesess a large number of interesting and famous castles, now mostly in ruins, and great mansions that the tourist can visit. For foreigners, probably the most famous castle in the country is Blarney.

This ancient castle is much the same as any other old Irish fortress that may be found throughout the country. It is a ruin, but a ruin in a good state of preservation. On the top levels, there is a wonderful view across lovely, undulating country, which is intersected by three rivers.

Blarney Castle, a fifteenth-century fortress

The castle itself is surrounded by old trees and wide, lush green fields. Because the roof has been destroyed for centuries, there are trees growing in the castle itself.

The great attraction is, of course, the famous Blarney Stone. Tradition has it that if you kiss the stone you will be given the gift of gab, which makes the flow of your speech so easy to listen to that no one will be able to resist your words.

The word "blarney" entered the language during the time of Queen Elizabeth I. Dermot McCarthy—Lord of Blarney Castle—was asked by the throne to surrender his fortress to Queen Elizabeth as a proof of his loyalty. He agreed, saying he would be delighted to prove himself in this, but was always stopped by unfortunate circumstances whenever he was finally about to do so. His excuses became so frequent

—but at the same time amusingly plausible—that they became a joke at the court. Her actual words are not recorded, but Queen Elizabeth is believed to have indignantly snorted something about "more Blarney talk," whereupon the word became a colorful part of the English vocabulary.

At one time, people who wished to kiss the Blarney Stone were held by their heels over the edge of the parapet while they fearfully puckered up for a kiss. When too many unfortunate accidents occurred, it was thought best to devise some other means of kissing the stone.

Today you sit down with your back to a steep drop of 150 feet. Your guide sits on your legs, holding your feet, and tells you to lie back over the drop and grasp two iron handrails. You find the legendary stone opposite your upside-down head and kiss it while hoping that your guide is not distracted from the business at hand. No one is sure of how the custom began.

Bunratty Castle and Folk Park

Today, the medieval banquet at Bunratty Castle is a high point for thousands of visitors to Ireland. When the banquet was first begun, an effort was made to see that the menus were authentically medieval. However, one of the customs of that time was that the dessert was served before the main course. Modern guests found this so objectionable that it had to be changed.

Another problem was the heavy use of saffron, which was very popular in the medieval period but now appeals only to a cultivated taste. Today, although the meal is contemporary in style, it still has a special quality because it is served without cutlery—in the traditional medieval manner.

The menu includes such dishes as "Henny's in Bruette" (Roast chicken); "Checkyns in Browet with Wortes" (Braised chicken with

Ancient Bunratty Castle, where medieval banquets are held throughout the year. The upper floors are furnished in a style that recreates the medieval atmosphere

vegetables and herbs); and, to finish off, "Syllabubs" plus "Berisin Syrippe."

The charming and very pretty hostesses tie aprons around the guests' necks and encourage them to make good use of their fingers. Otherwise, they don't eat! An exception is made for the dessert, when spoons are handed out. The drinks are mead, a delicious drink of fermented honey, and claret. Although this is an ancient Irish drink, it is now made only in Cornwall, in southern England.

Throughout the meal, a group of handsome young Irish people sing Irish folk songs, to which they accompany themselves with harps and fiddles.

Bunratty Castle stands on what was formerly the island of Trades on the northern shore of the Shannon River. The approach on the road from Limerick goes through farmlands that were once covered by the waters of the river. From the time of its construction during the Middle Ages, until the end of the eighteenth century, Bunratty was protected by its island position: it was washed by the tide and approachable only by a track that wandered down from the old road near Limerick.

Bunratty means the mouth of the Raite River—now called the O'Barney. Its strong position first attracted the Vikings, who had established a trading post at Limerick; it is believed that there is still some evidence of their hand in the construction of the shallow moat or ditch that surrounds the castle.

When the Normans arrived, they too saw the military advantages of the geographical situation; the first man to act on this was Robert de Muscegros, who in 1250 built a castle there. After De Muscegros' death, the lands were granted by the English king, Edward I, to Thomas de Clare, son of the Earl of Gloucester, who is 1277 rebuilt a much better and stronger castle. From that time on, the history of Bunratty is a stormy and violent chronicle of war, of many different owners and, finally, of decay and disuse.

As you look from the battlements of the castle today, there are not many buildings to be seen in the surrounding landscape (or were not until the recent development of the nearby folk village). But it is thought

Irish dancers and musicians entertain tourists in a cottage at Bunratty Folk Park

that during Norman times a village numbering about a thousand inhabitants surrounded the castle.

Bunratty Folk Park, adjacent to the castle, came into being in 1959. At that time, the introduction of jet planes made it necessary to lengthen the existing runways at Shannon Airport. In order to find enough land it was necessary to demolish a small farmhouse, which had stood on the site for perhaps two centuries. It was then that an imaginative person involved in the reconstruction of the airport realized that the contrast of this old house to the new development at Shannon would be of great interest to visitors to Ireland.

Eventually, ways and means were found to preserve this, as well as other old structures in the neighborhood. At first, the builders concentrated on the Tigh na Sionnaine (the Shannon Farmhouse). It was moved close to Bunratty Castle and furnished and fitted out as it would have been about the year 1900.

The planners were determined that everything within and outside the house be completely authentic; another objective was that the atmosphere not be the static and sometimes forbidding one of a museum but rather an informal and friendly one. Perhaps, it was reasoned, a woman of the house could be there to prepare a pot of tea and bake soda bread in a pot oven on the turf fire.

Powerscourt in County Wicklow is a magnificent eighteenth-century mansion with a view of Sugarloaf Mountain, exquisite formal gardens, a deer park, and a four-hundred-foot waterfall

This cottage proved so popular and attractive to tourists that other buildings of the traditional type in the area of the Shannon estuary were surveyed and reconstructed in what has become known as Bunratty Folk Park.

It was officially opened in July, 1964, when two small farmhouses, a fisherman's house, and a forge were put on display. Three other buildings have been added since, and there are plans to further enrich this folk heritage.

Bunratty Folk Park has no feeling of artifice about it; it is an excellent introduction to Irish folk art and country living.

Touring Estates

Ireland is full of beautiful old mansions that may be visited by the public. Westport House is one of the loveliest; it is owned by the Marquess of Sligo and was built in 1731 on the side of an old castle that had been constructed by an ancestor—the famous pirate queen of Connaught, Grace O'Malley.

The original castle dungeons still exist; they have now been "horrified," to the delight of visiting children. The house is a great repository of beautiful antique furniture, much of it dating from the eighteenth century. There are also gardens, a small chapel, and a lake on which you can boat. The Marquess of Sligo, his son, the Earl of Atamont, and his son's wife are frequently available to show tourists around, a gesture that greatly enhances the visitors' pleasure in the magnificent old house.

In several of the old mansions and castles live owners who cannot afford the expensive upkeep of these places. And yet, a previously opulent way of life, or respect for their family's traditions—or perhaps just a refusal to face the world outside—has induced many of these owners to cling to their estates, no matter how decayed they may be.

There is a story about one such eccentric who lived alone and made friends with the mice who had nests beneath the floors of his decaying mansion. Occasionally, while having a bit of a nip himself, he would give a drop to the mice as well. One day, when an English visitor came, one of the mice got drunk, stood up on its hind legs, and said,

"Call the dog in and I'll fight him." "How very extraordinary!" commented the English visitor. "Yes, it is, rather," the recluse replied. "Most often it's the cat he wants to fight."

Although no visitor to Ireland can begin to appreciate the country until they have visited the countryside, the Irish themselves—unlike the English—have no great fondness for country life.

Modern Attitudes Toward Country Life

Frank O'Connor writes that "to this day you will still not find what you find in almost every European country—the town-dweller who pines for a little place where he can garden and keep hens. In Ireland, the country represents poverty and ignorance. . . ."

It is true that, unlike the people of many other European nations, the Irish, because of the deprivations their rural people have suffered in the past, have little longing left for the charm and beauty of country living. The government has been concerned about the increasing flight of young men and women from the farms. In an effort to keep the farmers on the land, it has established Committees of Agriculture in each county, which offer courses in agriculture, forestry, and horticulture, to any person over eighteen living on a farm. Other courses offered are poultry keeping, dairying, and farm-related subjects. There is a special school at Cork that offers advanced training to young women, who become qualified instructors after taking these courses. They are expected to return home and pass their knowledge on to others.

Farms are small throughout the country, and in the west they are not only small but unproductive. Many farmers must work several months a year for someone else simply because the farms they own will not support them. For many farmers in the west of the country, life would be impossible without remittances from abroad which, in the middle and late sixties, were between $30 and $33 million a year.

The inevitable figure of all Irish country roads is the solitary man driving along slowly in his one-horse cart, with a large milk can (rarely more than two or three, as farms are small) rattling behind the driver's seat. At the local creamery—and most villages seem to have a creamery—the milk is separated. The farmer is paid for the cream, which is made into butter and either shipped to other markets, or sold locally. The skim milk is returned to the farmer, who uses it to feed his pigs.

On market days, the dairy farmer does not have the roads to himself —as he seems to much of the rest of the time. Market day is an important event in the Irish countryside. Before dawn, the squares become congested with animals and men—black Kerry cows, red-and-white shorthorns, calves and heifers, donkey carts, and soft-voiced, ruddy-cheeked men. The sheep are usually driven into town by boys and their dogs.

The cows, often splashed with mud, stand in the streets with dazed expressions on their faces, blocking traffic on the main street throughout the morning. Now and then an indignant shopekeeper comes

Peaceful, quiet scenes like this are common in the Irish countryside

out and smacks a cow out of the shop doorway. Such scenes are familiar to everyone in Ireland.

The average Irishman is only too glad to leave the farm, begin a new life in a town and never return (except for visits) to the harsh, boring life of the agricultural or pastoral poor. Perhaps this attitude will change as mechanization changes the character of country life. Already, industrialization has established an important beachhead in Shannon. Irish businessmen see it as only the beginning of a new way of life for the country.

Industrial Expansion

World-famous Shannon is situated in the idyllic western part of the island. Its prosperity began when the airport was built to accommodate the first transatlantic flights. For over ten years, all transatlantic

An aerial view of Shannon Industrial Zone, showing a frontal view of a standard factory unit and the airport runways in the rear

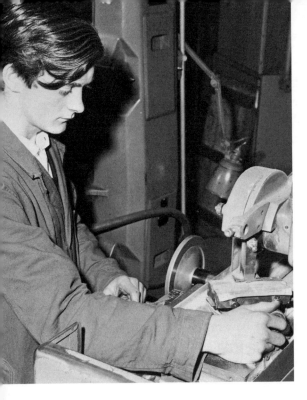

A young Irish worker learns new skills in a plant in the Industrial Zone

planes stopped for refueling at Shannon, and this in itself helped to create more interest in Ireland. Gradually, the area began to attract foreign investors, who erected factories and brought much-needed foreign capital into Ireland. Today Shannon is a fast-growing complex of industrial plants and apartment houses. Many of the industries are partly or completely owned by the British, American, Dutch, South African, and Japanese companies who have been attracted by the low labor costs and liberal tax concessions of the government. It is quite possible that Shannon may become the first industrial city of modern Ireland someday.

The growth of Irish International Airlines is one of the big success stories of the postwar period in Ireland. In April, 1936, Aer Lingus (Air Fleet) was formed with only $280,000 and twelve employees. Today it carries over a million passengers and sixteen thousand tons of freight a year. It operates the highest load factor on the Atlantic (72 percent of the seats are occupied by fare-paying passengers). Aer Lingus has become one of Ireland's major industries and is one of the most popular airlines between the United States and Europe.

Shannon International Airport was first opened to commercial transatlantic traffic in 1939. In those early days of air travel, when transatlantic flights were still somewhat risky, travelers were thrilled and relieved to see their plane, after a successful crossing, finally arrive in the safe haven of Shannon.

In 1947, a customs-free store was inaugurated, which quickly gained fame as an ideal place to buy quality products from all over the world at duty-free prices.

In the Republic of Ireland, industrial volume increased 84 percent from 1960 to 1969; agricultural output increased more than one third in the same period. Most large-scale industries were based mainly on native products, such as food and beverages, and textiles. The Guinness Brewery of Dublin is one of the top Irish companies. It ships 36,000,000 gallons of beer every year and is the world's largest exporter of this beverage.

Today, strong efforts toward diversification have partly succeeded. One reason Irish business has developed in recent years is the appearance of more imaginative Irishmen who have discovered that the Irish can succeed in the business world as well as anyone else.

Dermot Ryan is a good example of the new, enterprising young Irish businessman. While still at the university studying economics, Dermot decided to go into the car-rental business. For capital he used $225 he had earned selling advertising space for a university magazine and by peddling vegetables grown in his father's garden.

With this money he bought a fifteen-year-old Ford and opened an office over his father's pub in Portobello, a suburb of Dublin. Not being able to afford a desk, he used instead a makeshift arrangement of tea chests and planks. He couldn't even afford a telephone. When the advertisements he placed in Dublin papers brought inquiries from English vacationers (only one other firm was renting cars in Dublin at the time) the barman would thump on the ceiling with a broomstick so that Dermot could rush down to the bar to take the call. He did all the mechanical work himself and also acted as chauffeur when one was required. This happened in 1948. Ten years later, Dermot Ryan was a millionaire.

When Sybil Connolly opened a dressmaking establishment in Ireland in the late 1940's, there were no couturier shops whose creations could compare with her work. After the war, Sybil was discovered by American buyers, who helped promote her, and because of her unique and beautiful designs, her shop was turned into an establishment of international prestige.

Today Sybil Connolly employs fifty people in her workrooms and at least fifty more work in their own cottages making handwoven tweeds and hand-crocheted lace. Sybil Connolly's success has inspired other men and women to open dressmaking shops and high-level boutiques, and they have, in the process, helped to make Dublin become a clothes-design center.

Medical Care

Taxes take a good chunk out of wealthy people's income, but the government, if Ireland is to continue with its socialist programs, must have adequate revenue. Chief among these are the national health services.

Ireland is rapidly developing a national health service which will provide for the basic needs of all citizens. Already medical care is free for the lowest income group, which is estimated to comprise one third of the population. The middle group (estimated at about 55 percent) receives some free medical service, while those in the higher income must pay most of their own medical costs. The treatment of infectious diseases is free. (Cancer, especially lung cancer, since the Irish are heavy smokers, is the biggest cause of death.)

The average Irishman contributes to a government health-insurance plan and also to the social security system, which allows him half of his wage when he retires. Any family with children receives a government allowance, no matter what their income may be.

In the 1920's, Irish hospitals were faced with enormous financial problems. They tried to raise money by operating various lotteries and sweepstakes but were only moderately successful. Then a clever businessmen persuaded them to form a single national lottery that would offer very large prize money.

This was the beginning of the famous Irish Sweepstakes, which has provided nearly $200 million to Irish hospitals since the early 1930's. It is the state that distributes the funds; however the Sweepstakes are operated by a private business firm, which goes under the name of the Hospitals' Trust. Although the name has a charitable ring to it, this firm has actually grossed over a billion dollars because of the special privileges it enjoys, especially since the right to sell Sweepstakes tickets abroad was granted. Four fifths of the monies received are paid out in expenses, prizes, and profits—a fact that has drawn considerable

More than 200,000 pilgrims visit the Knock Shrine in County Mayo each year. An apparition of the Blessed Virgin Mary was reported here in 1879

criticism from those who know what a small percentage the hospitals actually receive. The November, 1966, issue of *Fortune* magazine suggested that the fraction that goes to the hospitals is "probably less than the company would have had to pay in normal corporate taxes, were it not given official exemption."

Change Is in the Air

Such a situation would seem to call for change—and change is in the air in Ireland. Irish students do not riot, but they thoughtfully question concepts the older generation held absolutely and unconditionally right. Like so many Irish generations before them, they are patient and have great respect for authority, but nevertheless they are far more aware of the outside world than their parents were—and they are questioning the old Irish values.

There is an amusing story that illustrates the change of young people's attitudes, but its authenticity has not been verified. It tells of a priest who noticed a young girl from his parish wearing a brief bikini. Greatly disturbed, he at once sent the girl a note requesting her to wear a one-piece bathing suit. Her quick reply asked, "Which piece do you want me to take off?"

For all stories regarding such changes, there are just as many that are contradictory. When the Archbishop of Dublin came home after the final session of the Vatican Ecumenical Council in Rome, he told his congregation, "You may have been worried by much talk of changes to come. Allow me to reassure you. No change will worry the tranquillity of your Christian lives."

Such remarks are exactly what church liberals have come to expect from the Catholic hierarchy; they are weary of the reactionary character of the Irish Catholic Church. Yet, small changes have been made and are continuing to be made. Now Mass is being said in English or Irish instead of in Latin. Even marriages between Catholics and Protestants are not the disaster that they inevitably became when such bonds were formed in the past.

Critics of the Church believe that its emphasis continues to be on

A wayside pump wrapped for protection from freezing. Most farms now have running water, but in remote areas such pumps are still in use

matters of doctrine and theology; they are impatient with its reluctance to face pressing contemporary matters. They sense the growing climate of change in Ireland and want the Church to be in the forefront of what is to come.

A Peaceful Revolution

Undoubtedly, a great surge of self-confidence and pride arose in the Irish people when John Fitzgerald Kennedy became President of the United States. Few people realized that at the time of his inauguration he was following, perhaps unconsciously, an ancient Irish tradition by inviting the distinguished American poet Robert Frost to read a poem, especially written for the inauguration. (According to this ancient custom, a poet must be present at the coronation of the high king.)

In 1963, when he visited the homeland of his great-grandparents, President Kennedy said, "In the years since independence, you have undergone a new, a peaceful revolution, an economic and industrial revolution, transforming the face of this land, while still holding to the old spiritual and cultural values. You have modernized your economy, harnessed your rivers, diversified your industry, liberalized your trade, electrified your farms, accelerated your rate of growth and improved the living standard of your people . . . other nations in the world in whom Ireland has long invested her people and her children are now investing their capital as well as their vacations in Ireland . . . this revolution is not yet over. . . . This has never been a rich or powerful country, and yet, since earliest times, its influence on the world has been rich and powerful. No larger nation did more to keep Christianity and

A peat-fired generator to supply electricity to farms in the area rises out of the flat midlands

Western culture alive in their darkest centuries. No larger nation did more to spark the cause of independence in America, indeed, around the world. And no larger nation has ever provided the world with more literary and artistic genius. This is an extraordinary country."

That it is extraordinary has become increasingly clear to many foreign artists and writers and other creative workers who have found Ireland a peaceful haven in which to work when the complexities of life in their own countries became too difficult. The American film director John Huston, who has an estate in the west of Ireland, said, "I love Ireland. I love living there. It's rich and amusing. There's a wonderful way of life there, way behind the times, thank Christ. It's kind of pre-Civil War. People stay in each other's houses, and hunting takes precedence over everything else." (Huston has since become an Irish citizen and now serves as joint master of the Galway Blazers, a century-old hunt club.)

Writer John Steinbeck often went to Ireland, where he found the atmosphere conducive for his writing.

When Charles de Gaulle stepped down from the presidency of France in 1969, he chose Ireland to vacation in; his staff and family occupied a country inn for a month—much to the delight of the Irish Tourist Board.

Dreaming and Reality

In George Bernard Shaw's play, *John Bull's Other Island,* an embittered Irishman named Doyle exclaims;

> Oh, the dreaming! The dreaming!
> The torturing, heartscaling, never
> satisfying dreaming, dreaming, dreaming!
> No debauchery that ever coarsened and
> brutalized an Englishman can take the
> worth and usefulness out of him like
> that of dreaming.
> An Irishman's imagination never lets him
> alone, never convinces him, never satisfies

him; but it makes him that he can't face
reality nor deal with it nor handle it nor
conquer it . . .

But dreaming is no longer as important to the Irishman of today;
his thoughts are practical ones, concerned with better jobs, with
education for his children, with housing, and with learning more about
what is going on in the rest of the world. No longer are the Irish com-
placent about their spirituality, which was commonly believed, in times
past, to surpass that of other nations; the ecumenical spirit has reached
Ireland too. The Irish of today also realize that Western Europe has
made enormous strides in technology, in social welfare, and the arts,
and that if they are ever to catch up, they must hurry.

Dromoland Castle in its fairyland setting of parks, lakes, and rolling hills is a re-
minder of the past

Those who love Ireland hope it *can* catch up without destroying its unique charm and beauty. The Irish still do not fish their bountiful seas, the Irish cow gives only half as much milk as do cows in other countries; there is a strong tendency to be sociable while at work. Will Irishmen be able to increase productivity and still retain all the qualities that make them such a remarkable people? This is only one of the many questions that must be worked out in the years to come.

Such considerations make Ireland an interesting place. The very strength of the past giving way to change and ferment, the confrontation of centuries-old prejudices with new beliefs—these are always thrilling events; in Ireland the interplay of such conflicting forces may even be more compelling. Certainly they will be as unpredictable and contradictory as the mysterious—and charming—Irish spirit.

Reading List

The Crock of Gold, by James Stephens. New York: The Macmillan Company, 1960.

Cry Blood, Cry Erin, by Redmond Fitzgerald. New York: Clarkson N. Potter, Inc., 1966.

Dublin: A Portrait, by V. S. Pritchett. Photographs by Evelyn Hofer. New York: Harper & Row, 1967.

Enjoying Ireland, by William and Constance Kehoe. New York: The Devin-Adair Company, 1966.

Finnegans Wake, by James Joyce. New York: The Viking Press, 1959.

The Great Hunger, by Cecil Woodham-Smith. New York: Harper & Row, 1963.

The Improbable Irish, by Walter Bryan. New York: Taplinger Publishing Co., Inc., 1969.

The Indestructible Irish, by John Philip Cohane. New York: Meredith Press, 1969.

Inishfallen, Fare Thee Well, by Sean O'Casey. New York: The Macmillan Company, 1960.

Ireland, by Joe McCarthy. New York: Life World Library, 1964.

The Irish, by Donald S. Connery. New York: Simon & Schuster, 1968.

The Irish: A Character Study, by Sean O'Faolain. New York: The Devin-Adair Company, 1949.

The Irish Answer, by Tony Gray. Boston: Little, Brown & Company, 1966.

Irish Roundabout, by Isla Mitchell. New York: Dodd, Mead & Company, 1952.

John Bull's Other Island, by George Bernard Shaw. London: Constable & Company, Ltd., 1947.

Life in Ireland, by Louis M. Cullen. New York: G. P. Putnam's Sons, 1969.

Out of the Lion's Paw: Ireland Wins Her Freedom, by Constantine Fitz-Gibbon. Visual material collected by George Morrison. New York: American Heritage Publishing Co., Inc., 1969.

The Playboy of the Western World, by John M. Synge. Edited by Henry Popkin. New York: Avon Books, 1967.

The Plough and the Stars, by Sean O'Casey. New York: St. Martin's Press, 1966.

Portrait of the Artist as a Young Man: Text and Criticism, edited by Chester G. Anderson. New York: The Viking Press, 1968.

Shell Guide to Ireland, by Lord Killanin and Michael V. Duignan. New York: W. W. Norton & Company, 1967.

The Yeats Country, compiled by Sheelah Kirby. Chester Springs, Pennsylvania: Dufour Editions, 1963.

Highlights in Irish History

B.C.

6000 First settlement of Ireland by Mesolithic—Middle Stone Age—hunters.

A.D.

254 Cormac Mac Art, High King of Tara.

432 St. Patrick arrives in Ireland.

795 First Viking raid on Ireland.

1014 Brian Boru breaks the Norse power at the Battle of Clontarf.

1170 Norman invasion of Ireland.

1366 The Statutes of Kilkenny enacted in an effort to keep the Anglo-Normans separate from the conquered Irish.

1394 Richard II of England lands in Ireland with a large army.

1541 Anglo-Irish parliament acknowledges Henry VIII of England as King (instead of Lord) and head of the Church of Ireland. Suppression of the monasteries follows.

1591 Foundation of Trinity College, Dublin.

1607 The flight of the Earls (O'Neill and O'Donnell) opens the way for the plantation of Ulster with Protestant settlers.

1649 Oliver Cromwell subdues Ireland.

1690 The Battle of the Boyne.

1695 Penal Laws enacted against the Catholic population.

1798 Nationwide insurrection planned by the United Irishmen is defeated. Theobald Wolfe Tone dies.

1800 Act of Union with Great Britain. Irish parliament in Dublin is dissolved.

1803 Robert Emmet's abortive insurrection fails.

1829 Daniel O'Connell wins Catholic Emancipation.

1846–47 The failure of the potato crop causes the Great Famine. Population of Ireland ultimately reduced by death and immigration from about eight million to four million.

1848 The Young Ireland leaders make an abortive attempt at insurrection.

1858	The Irish Republic Brotherhood (Fenian movement) is founded in Ireland and by exiles in America.
1905	Sinn Fein movement founded by Arthur Griffith.
1912	Irish Home Rule Bill passed by British House of Commons is due to come into effect in 1914; but its provisions are defied by the Ulster volunteers. Bill suspended for duration of the First World War.
1916	Easter Week Uprising; proclamation of the Irish Republic. The insurrection is crushed after four days.
1921	Treaty with Britain, establishing the Irish Free State of 26 counties. Civil War between Free-Staters and Republicans follows.
1926	Republicans led by Eamon de Valera form the Fianna Fáil party.
1939	Ireland remains neutral during the Second World War.
1949	The 26 counties secede from the British Commonwealth and become a sovereign state, the Republic of Ireland.
1955	The Republic of Ireland joins the United Nations.
1957	Eamon de Valera again elected *Taoiseach* (Prime Minister).
1961	Ireland enters UNESCO.
1964	Ireland sends troops to serve with United Nations forces in Cyprus.
1968	Violence erupts in Northern Ireland.

214

Index

About the Author

ARNOLD DOBRIN has long been a compulsive traveler. He journeyed to Japan, Thailand, Italy, and Canada in search of "fresh revelations" resulting in four storybooks illustrated by Mr. Dobrin for young readers. During his two-year stay in Rome, he also wrote *Italy: Modern Renaissance,* which was well received by critics and readers, who enjoyed Mr. Dobrin's informed observations and comments. His curiosity and artist's eye inevitably note the most vivid and sensuous details, which are interwoven with the history and traditions of the country he is writing about.

In recent years he has also produced two distinguished biographies—*Aaron Copland: His Life and Times;* and *Igor Stravinsky: His Life and Times.* Mr. Dobrin lives in Westport, Connecticut, with his wife and two young sons.

World Neighbors

Written to introduce the reader to his contemporaries in other lands and to sketch the background needed for an understanding of the world today, these books are well-documented, revealing presentations. Based on first-hand knowledge of the country and illustrated with unusual photographs, the text is informal and inviting. Geographical, historical, and cultural data are woven unobtrusively into accounts of daily life. Maps, working index, chronology, and bibliography are useful additions.

ALASKA Pioneer State, by Norma Spring
THE ARAB MIDDLE EAST, by Larry Henderson
ARGENTINA, PARAGUAY & URUGUAY, by Axel Hornos
AUSTRALIA & NEW ZEALAND, by Lyn Harrington
AUSTRIA & SWITZERLAND Alpine Countries, by Bernadine Bailey
BRAZIL Awakening Giant, by Kathleen Seegers
CANADA Young Giant of the North, by Adelaide Leitch
CENTRAL AMERICA Lands Seeking Unity, by Charles Paul May
CHILE Progress on Trial, by Charles Paul May
CHINA & THE CHINESE, by Lyn Harrington
CZECHOSLOVAKIA, HUNGARY, POLAND, by Ivan & Mary Volgyes
EQUATORIAL AFRICA New World of Tomorrow, by Glenn Kittler
GERMANY A Divided Nation, by Alma & Edward Homze
GREECE & THE GREEKS, by Lyn Harrington
INDIA Land of Rivers, by L. Winifred Bryce
IRELAND The Edge of Europe, by Arnold Dobrin
ISRAEL New People in an Old Land, by Lily Edelman
ITALY Modern Renaissance, by Arnold Dobrin
JAPAN Crossroads of East and West, by Ruth Kirk
THE LOW COUNTRIES Gateways to Europe, by Roland Wolseley
MEDITERRANEAN AFRICA Four Muslim Nations, by Glenn Kittler
MEXICO Land of Hidden Treasure, by Ellis Credle
PERU, BOLIVIA, ECUADOR The Indian Andes, by Charles Paul May
SCANDINAVIA The Challenge of Welfare, by Harvey Edwards
THE SOVIET UNION A View from Within, by Franklin Folsom
SPAIN & PORTUGAL Iberian Portrait, by Daniel Madden
THE UNITED KINGDOM A New Britain, by Marian Moore
VIETNAM and Countries of the Mekong, by Larry Henderson
THE WEST INDIES Islands in the Sun, by Wilfred Cartey
YUGOSLAVIA, ROMANIA, BULGARIA, by Lila Perl

HETERICK MEMORIAL LIBRAR
941.5 D634i
Dobrin, Arnold/Ireland: the edge of Euro

3 5111 00024 5104

Heterick Memorial Library
Ohio Northern University
Ada, Ohio 45810